# Confucius Without Confusion:

## Between Individualism and Social Harmony

**Everett Ofori**

Copyright © 2023 by Everett Ofori

All rights reserved. No part of this publication may be reproduced, stored in a retrieval system, or transmitted, in any form or by any means, without the prior permission in writing of Everett Ofori (everettoforijapan@gmail.com), or as expressly permitted by law, or under terms agreed with the appropriate reprographics rights organization.

ISBN-13: 978-1-894221-17-7
ISBN-10: 1-894221-17-6

# Acknowledgments

I have often heard people that I admire speak about the humanities as being crucial to acquiring a well-rounded education. I could not agree more. Though I believe I have so much more to read and learn, my experience in the Humanities (HUX) program at California State University (Dominguez Hills), USA, with the help of superb instructors such as Dr. Debra Best, Dr. Daniel Greenspan, Dr. Iset Anuakan, Dr. David A. Churchman, Dr. Christopher Monty, Dr. Kimberly Bohman-Kalaja, and Dr. William Hagan, helped me think along fresh new lines.

Support also came from Dr. Matthew Luckett and Dr. Emily Magruder who helped shepherd me through the all-important but sticky administrative details connected with the Humanities Program.

Final thanks to Ms. Brigette Brown for her patient assistance in helping me through the final formatting formalities and to Mr. Charles Acquah for the benefit of his keen eye for design, which has served me well on several occasions.

# TABLE OF CONTENTS

| | |
|---|---|
| ACKNOWLEDGMENTS | 5 |
| PREFACE | 9 |
| 1. INTRODUCTION | 11 |
| 2. CONFUCIUS: THE MAN AND HIS TIME | 18 |
| 3. INDIVIDUALISM UNDERPINS THE COMMUNITARIAN SPIRIT | 24 |
| 4. INDIVIDUALISM IN RECOGNITION OF THE EQUAL WORTH OF ALL HUMAN BEINGS | 37 |
| 5. INDIVIDUALISM AND THE HARD ROAD TOWARDS SELF-CULTIVATION. | 42 |
| 6. BECOMING A PERSON OF VIRTUE: LEARNING TO STAND ALONE | 56 |
|     Benevolence/Humaneness (*ren*) | 57 |
|     Desire | 63 |
|     Timeliness | 68 |
|     Filial piety (*xiao*) | 70 |
|     Ritual Propriety/Ritual (*li*) | 74 |
|     Flexibility | 78 |
|     Loyalty (*zhong*) | 79 |
|     Self-reflection (*shu*) | 82 |
|     Wisdom (*zhi*) | 85 |
| 7. INDIVIDUALISM IN THE DIVERGENT PERSPECTIVES OF CONFUCIANISTS | 88 |

8. THE MATTER OF INDIVIDUAL
   RESPONSIBILITY . . . 108
9. THE INDIVIDUAL'S
   RELATIONSHIP TO THE FAMILY   115
10. CONFUCIAN HIERARCHY,
    LEADERSHIP, AND
    INDIVIDUALISM . . . 122
11. WOMEN, CONFUCIANISM, AND
    INDIVIDUALITY . . . 137
12. CONFUCIANISM AND CREATIVE
    AUTONOMY . . . . 147
13. CHALLENGES TO THE CONFUCIAN
    NOTION OF INDIVIDUALISM . 153
14. CONCLUSION . . . . 161

WORKS CITED . . . . 164

CHRONOLOGY OF CHINESE
    DYNASTIES . . . . 173

INDEX . . . . . . 174

ABOUT THE AUTHOR . . . 182

# Preface

It has become an article of faith that Confucianism is synonymous with communitarianism. Few people are aware, however, that this strong characterization, evident as it appears on the surface, was in part, an image that was imposed on Chinese society by such Western scholars as Max Weber to distinguish it from Western society.

While the intention seems to have been an attempt to uphold the superiority of the West over the East, i.e., individualism over communitarianism, in recent years, scholars such as Harvard's Michael Sandel, see the supposed communitarianism of Confucian society as being more positive than the individualism of the West, where each person stands alone. This book examines Confucian society in great detail and reveals that while indeed there were features of communitarianism in Confucian society, there was also the tendency towards individual agency in the choices people made towards their life's work, their autonomy to develop their talents either as scholars or artists, and their willingness to undergo the privations of solitude and perpetual study, not necessarily for personal gain but to make themselves useful stewards of the truth.

In addition, Confucian scholars were not just pliable bookworms; they could use their gifts and the fruits of their self-cultivation in service of their society.

# CHAPTER 1
# INTRODUCTION

Many scholarly discussions of Confucianism today note how integral communitarianism was to that philosophy, with some explicitly noting that it was a philosophy devoid of individualism (Rosemont xiv), and that, Confucianism does not see fellow human beings as "autonomous individuals, but as fundamentally role-bearers, who live those roles, not merely 'play' them" (xiv). Since Westerners see individualism as a virtue, Rosemont hastens to add that the supposed lack of individualism in Confucianism is not meant to be a shortcoming, but rather "a strength of their position" (9). Rosemont suggests that the community-oriented perspective that is tied to Confucianism, though meant to be negative, might be more positive than Western writers seem to understand.

Another researcher, Chad Hansen, has explicitly stated that there is no individuality in Chinese culture (Brindley xviii), and current accounts of people from Chinese cultural backgrounds, seem to bear witness to the importance they place on family and the respect they show for community harmony above personal independence. Rather than wade into the debate on individualism versus communitarianism, psychologist David Y. F. Ho offers that, Confucianism might better be characterized as having "relationship dominance" (116). In other words, Confucianism prized human relationships. Confucian society was primed to think about the Five Cardinal Relationships: "between ruler and minister, between father and son, between husband and wife, between brothers, and between friends" (116). But this did not mean total rejection of the individual as an entity. Ho further suggests that Confucianists do not act so much from personal need or will as from the constant awareness of their interdependent relationships.

Evidence in the modern day, in countries such as Japan, the two Koreas, and Singapore, all of which have been steeped in Confucianism for ages, and where group harmony is highly valued, lends credence to the depths to which Confucian society has historically appeared to elevate community over the individual. This book, therefore, does not challenge the presence of a spirit of communitarianism under Confucianism. The promotion of such a communitarian spirit within Confucianism does not appear to have been for any evil purposes, such as the enslavement of the individual or an attempt to hold back individual development. Rather, the strong predilection towards attachment to community, simply recognized that there are goods in society that might be better obtained through special human relationships

(Tan, Confucius 215). That is, in a world where want and poverty were real, the need for families to stick close to one another for support might not have been a difficult sell.

In Chinese society more broadly, and Confucianism in particular, the focus on the family was a central tenet (Stockman 95). This was the primary basis and the first step for an individual's attachment to others. But even this primary attachment does not spring out of nothingness, for children that are taught to respect their parents had first been catered to and nurtured from infancy. And the encouragement of some measure of reciprocity in the child's relationship with those in their immediate family was certainly not an attempt to strip the child of their individuality; it was an acknowledgment that the child, that individual, was important enough to respect and to embrace, and that it was only fair for the child to similarly embrace this spirit of mutual concern for one another.

According to Erica Brindley, a cultural historian of early China (500 BC to 200 CE), a defining characteristic of Confucianism was that individual obligations were so geared towards fulfilling the needs of the family that they tended to eclipse the individual (xi). The self could not be untethered from the community since the self was developed through support from the community in the form of parents and teachers and other entities to which the individual had to relate (Kolstad and Gjesvik 255-256). Thus, the individual, according to Charlene Tan, an educationist and philosopher of education, "is always constituted through a community that exists in shared social and cultural understandings, traditions, and practices" (Tan, "For group" 479). In effect, the individual is socialized from the very beginning to appreciate family ties and to build a measure of commitment to it. This socialization, in many cultures, is found in the proverbs, maxims, and aphorisms that children hear from their earliest years. It was no different in the Confucian household.

In the communitarian society linked to Confucianism, the individual, having been imbued with the values of the community, has an obligation to the society that gave birth to their moral sensibilities. In effect, one constituted within a communitarian value system contributes "to society by supporting his or her community and adhering to a set of publicly shared values" (Tan 480). There is ample support for those who see Confucian societies primarily in communitarian terms (De Bary, Asian Values 8; Kim, Confucianism, Law, & Democracy 151). According to Hu Weixi, communitarian ideas were prevalent in Pre-Qin Confucianism and advanced to the point of becoming a systematic theory through the learning of the "four books," namely *The Great Learning, Doctrine of the Mean, Analects,* and *Mencius* (475).

Even so, while it is true that adherents of Confucianism valued respect for hierarchy and harmony in the community, Brindley notes that Mencius and Yang Zhu, two key figures in the Confucian world, actually represented the rise of individualism in early China (126). Thus, while communitarianism is part of Confucianism, the philosophy is misunderstood for its supposed lack of individualism. This is a matter that needs reconsideration as the Confucian aim of creating a harmonious society could not have been possible without leaving room for individualism. After all, communitarianism without free choice sounds like an environment steeped in coercion or tyranny.

There are many different ways in which the idea of individualism might be interpreted. Confucianism did not need to represent all the different strains of individualism to be recognized as a philosophy that was open to individual agency. This book, therefore, acknowledges that, indeed, Confucianism had a communitarian strand that sought to bring about harmony in society; more than that, Confucianism acknowledged the "equality" of all human beings, supported self-development as far as the individual wished to go, the individual's right to autonomous decision-making, and meritocracy that recognized human agency, all recognized elements of individualism.

The emphasis placed on communitarianism seems

to have emerged from Western scholars who sought to create a kind of Chinese identity that contrasted with that of the West. These scholars, according to Brindley, presented a positive view of individualism that is tied to such notions as human rights within an "exclusively European and American" sphere (ix), while "pointing to China's deep involvement with Confucian values as defining individual obligations to one's family so as to overshadow the importance of the self" (x).

This skewed view seems to have become widespread, in part because of Max Weber, whose views about the individual in ancient China is described by Brindley as having been both misleading and based on "a biased method of inquiry" (xvii). Weber, it seems, simply set China up as a negative contrast to Enlightenment Europe, the subject that he sought to promote. As research bears out, not only did Confucianism support a measure of individuality but also the notion of individuality was a subject of intense discussion among Confucianists and thinkers and philosophers of other contemporary schools of thought of the day such as Daoism and Mohism (Brindley 1, 77).

The next chapter provides some background on the world in which Confucianism emerged, its chief figures, and the main texts that argued for the existence of individuality in a world of communitarian Confucianism.

# *Notes*

# CHAPTER 2
# CONFUCIUS: THE MAN AND HIS TIME

To understand Confucianism, it is necessary to understand the writings and the key figures who have come to represent this philosophy. Confucius, who lived around 551-479 BCE, is perhaps China's most well-known sage. He was a thinker whose interests embraced both the needs of the individual and the concerns of society, including its political leadership.

Confucianism touched a wide array of values and practices that were linked to a concern for morality (Littlejohn xix), and Confucius thought of himself not as the originator of the key ideas associated with him, but more as a "transmitter of tradition" (De Bary, The Trouble with Confucianism 3). This was a role in which Confucius was particularly proud, and one that also positioned him as someone who was not just trying to be popular. His wisdom, his gifts as a teacher, his conduct and his modesty made him a role model for the community.

Knowledge of Confucius and his teachings comes to us chiefly through the *Analects*, a collection of his purported sayings, in which Confucius is presented as being in conversation with various students. Besides Confucius, others are depicted as teachers in this volume of twenty chapters. In the *Analects*, Confucius shines as a moralist, and as one eager to share with his followers the importance of ethical living rather than attachment to wealth or honor. Confucius himself referred to legendary figures such as Emperor Yao and Emperor Shun as examples of virtuous living. Thus, "the idea of the sage-king was Chinese before it became Confucian" (De Bary, The Trouble with Confucianism 3). In particular, in terms of its history, culture, and literature, Confucius considered the Zhou dynasty (1045 BCE-256 BCE) as a period that had successfully held on to wisdom from earlier sages and kings. Confucius lived through the period known as the Spring and Autumn Period (722-481 BCE) (Ames and Rosemont 14) and made it his life's goal to share with others what he considered to be the most fitting teachings about government and good conduct.

Chinese legend has it that the earliest stages of Chinese life lay in three sage-kings called Yao, Shun, and Yu and their respective three dynasties, namely, the Xia (2070-1600 BCE), the Shang (1600-1300 BCE, early phase), and (1300-1046 BCE, later phase), and the Zhou (1040-771 BCE) (Coward, Neufeldt, and Neumaier 249). The Zhou dynasty existed in the Western part of China in what is now known as Xi'an. In 771 BCE, a civil war started over disagreements with kingly succession. The winners of the encounter moved the capital towards the east, which became the Eastern Zhou dynasty (770-221 BCE). This same period is broken into the Spring and Autumn Period (722-481 BCE) and the Warring States Period (c. 480-221 BCE) (Littlejohn 1). In such an uncertain era, while some leaders distinguished themselves on the battlefield, others in the society, such as Confucius, sought to advance philosophies and ways of thinking that would translate into a peaceful, well-ordered society.

Confucius often shared with his followers his admiration of King Wen, the founder of Zhou, and his son, who became victorious over the Shang dynasty. Another person that Confucius admired from the Zhou dynasty period was the Duke of Zhou, whom Confucius considered a paragon of virtue and an exemplar. As he says in the *Analects*, "How I have gone downhill! It has been such a long time since I dreamt of the Duke of Zhou" (Confucius 7.5). The reason for Confucius's admiration of the Duke of Zhou was the duke's apparent honesty in having served as a regent for his nephew, the son of his elder brother, and for not having taken over or "stolen" the throne. Throughout his life, Confucius sought to hold up to his followers this image of the value of the virtuous life even as he denied that he was the perfect image of it.

Confucius, who has captured the imagination of successive generations of Chinese and non-Chinese alike, was a lover of learning who had immersed himself in the thoughts, ideas, and writings that had come down from earlier generations. This included poems and historical documents as well as ritual instructions, customs, and traditions (Littlejohn 4). In fact, in the early part of the Zhou dynasty, a professional class of scholars had emerged, called the *Ru*. These scholars, who dated back sixty generations before Confucius, were considered counselors (Ames and Rosemont 106) that had taken it upon themselves to teach the people and guide them.

Confucius saw himself in this mold and urged his followers to be "a *Ru* of an exemplary person *(junzi ru)* but to avoid being a *Ru* for a petty person" (Confucius 6.13). The *Ru* had to learn a wide range of subjects and those who reflected the best forms of the tradition could serve as examples to others. And yet, not even Confucius himself hoped to be a master of all of the subjects at their disposal. Becoming a *Ru* was a lifetime endeavor to continue improving oneself. They had to handle not only religious rituals and political ceremonies but also be adept in divination, dance, music, archery, poetry, and geomancy (Littlejohn 5). The *Ru* made their living by serving as consultants to various rulers and officials. Also, they took on private students (5). Confucius, for his part, sought always to guide his followers towards what was high-minded and noble, and to take their minds away from the ignoble and the crass.

A few of the books that existed in the world in which Confucius was born include the *I Ching* or *Book of Changes*; *Hsiao Ching* or *The Book of Filial Piety*; the *Shu Ching* or the *Book of History*; the *Shi Ching* or the *Book of Odes*; and *Li Chi* or the *Book of Ceremonies* (Dawson xiv).

There was also *The Great Learning* (*Daxue*) and the *Doctrine of the Mean* (*Zhongyong*). These latter two books, in particular, were memorized by children whose families wanted them to have an education. *The Great Learning* and the *Doctrine of the Mean* were part of a larger volume and it is believed that the former was written by a junior disciple of Confucius known as Zeng Shen (505-436 BC) while the *Doctrine of the Mean* was written by Zisi, a grandson of Confucius. These two books were frequently cited by Mencius, one of the most important successors of Confucius, as authorities. Also, The *Six Classics* that were required for the training of scholars were as follows: the *Classic of Poetry*, the *Classic of History*, the *Classic of Rites,* the *Classic of Music,* the *Classic of Changes*, and the *Spring and Autumn An-*

*nals.* In addition to counseling rulers, the *Ru* took on the role of models and guides for the masses, a North Star that might guide the ordinary people into expressing the nobler aspects of their personality.

The next section explains how the communitarian aspect of Confucianism is underpinned by individualism.

## *Notes*

# CHAPTER 3
# INDIVIDUALISM UNDERPINS THE COMMUNITARIAN SPIRIT

The concept of individualism has traditionally been associated with the Western intellectual tradition whereas the East has often been seen as collectivist in orientation, one in which the individual must bow to the dictates of the society. While Max Weber had sought to elevate the West and its association with individualism and democracy, since the 1980s, novel voices, including Alasdair MacIntyre (1929-), Michael Sandel (1953-), and Charles Taylor (1931-), recasting their gaze upon "the individual as an independent subject with no relation to the community" (Lee, Confucianism 89) as something negative, sought to elevate the communitarianism associated with China and Confucianism as a positive worldview.

In exploring the concept of individualism, it is good

to consider how individualism is manifest so that we can better determine if any of the strains of individualism that scholars recognize can be found within Confucian philosophy. As sociology professor Steven Lukes notes, the concept of individuality is far from being precise; there are many different manifestations of it, including autonomy, self-direction, privacy, self-development, equality, and freedom (1).

A person who decides, of his own free will, to follow in his father's footsteps because of the realization that what he has learned throughout the years from his father fits him into a useful position in the society will be exercising autonomy just as the individual who decides that having weighed the options at his disposal, he would rather chart a different path from the work the family has been doing over the years. In both cases, as long as there is no undue coercion beyond what might be properly considered the provision of advice by someone with greater experience than the youth, people who make such choices can be viewed as having exercised personal discretion. There is no indication that Confucianism sought to put obstacles in the way of people exercising their agency, whether in marriage, occupation, or avocation. There is also no indication that Confucianism compelled people to follow set paths in life.

Further, in exploring the meaning of individualism, philosopher and sociologist Georg Simmel, notes that individualism must of necessity relate to some other world in ways that are either "practical or ideal, negative or affirmative, ruling or subservient, indifferent or passionate" (67). In other words, it is possible on one scale of individualism for people to not concern themselves with the lives of others. That is, in essence, to live a self-contained life free from "entanglements" with others. But then, on the other hand, there are those for whom individuality is still more meaningful because they view their lives in comparison with those of others. Such an individual "experiences both an inner centeredness, self-sufficiency and a world of his or her own, and a relationship, positive or negative to a totality in which he or she belongs, whether in adherence to it or detachment from it…" (69).

In the lives of outstanding Confucianists such as Mencius, Zisi, Cheng Hao, and others, we see individuals who were able to devote time and energy towards fulfilling the personal urge for self-development. But they all tied this concentration on the self to serving members of the societies to which they belonged, thus fitting into the latter portrayal of individualism noted earlier by Simmel.

Those who chose the path of the scholar-official had to prepare for rigorous examinations that took years of study, an endeavor that would no doubt require not only self-direction but also periods of solitude and privacy as they sought to master the official texts. This aspect of Confucianism, it appears, fits in very well with the characterization of individualism posited by sociologist John O'Brien, who admits in his research on culture, ethnography, inequality, race, identity, religion, and Islam, to the multivalent nature of individualism. O'Brien notes that three of the key characteristics of individualism are voluntarism, self-actualization, and privatization (174). Artistic pursuits, for example, such as those that Confucian scholars engaged in, required years of practice, self-direction, and some measure of privacy for practitioners to achieve mastery. The scholarly life, if forced upon a person, could not be sustained; it requires the use of enormous mental energy over decades. A person forced into that life against their will is likely to fall by the wayside sooner or later.

Scholars who have failed to see individualism in Confucian society might have been measuring the idea of individuality by a yardstick rooted in Western notions of a person who not only seeks their path in life but aims to do so without any concern for contributing to the society that bred and nurtured them. If so, then the notion of individualism in traditional Chinese society might not accord fully with that of the Western intellectual tradition, but that would not mean that individualism was wholly absent from Chinese society or from the Confucian tradition that has been the dominant mode of thinking and way of life in China from the sixth century B.C. to today.

Strains of individualism in Confucianism can be found further in the quest for self-cultivation, which required determination and sacrifice that stretched over a lifetime. It is found further in human agency, which was explicated by Mencius, one of the key figures in Confucianism, and respect for meritocracy, which acknowledged that individuals could transcend the strictures of social status to enter the highest social and political strata. In effect, the Western concept of individualism, which Brindley characterizes as an individual who owes "nothing to society" (Brindley xi), was not the kind of individualism that ran through Confucian society. Rather, Confucian individualism focuses on how individuals can achieve their goals while maintaining important relationships with others. It is not a matter of trying so hard to extricate oneself from relationships with others in order to appreciate one's sense of individuality (Brindley xii). Confucianism offered those who committed to it an opportunity to understand the self, and to shape that self into a person that was useful not only to the self but also to those around. In fact, it seems that the kind of learning that helped to foster such a sense of responsibility was one in which learning was a delight, not one of indoctrination. It was the kind of learning that a person would do not because of potential monetary gain but for the sake of knowledge acquisition and self-improvement.

As De Bary explains, this should not be taken as a radical individualism which asserts its complete autonomy "but of a Confucian personalism which affirms the importance of the self or person (*shen* or *tsu*) as the dynamic center of a larger social whole" (De Bary, "Neo-Confucian Individualism" 332). De Bary & Bloom explain further that even though all human beings share some commonalities, each is distinct in constitution as well as capacities, and as such, one needs to examine what is right and wrong for oneself, not just accept what others say. Such an approach of learning for one's self, which was fully supported by Confucianism, meant "allowing no self-deception, and this is true for all—common person and sage" (Sources of Chinese Tradition 871). Under Confucianism, sages and others learned that people could earn respect, but they were certainly not to be worshipped.

The people who surrounded Confucius found joy in the precepts he imparted, including the value of ritual, which is primarily community-oriented (Tu, Humanity & Self-cultivation 201); self-cultivation, which has both elements of individuality and community (Ivanhoe, Confucian Moral Self-Cultivation 1); and proper behavior, which also depends on individual orientation towards the community (Chan, "Confucian ethics" 248).

But, as an instructor, Confucius's relationship with his direct followers was not one of a sage on the stage throwing pearls of wisdom at his students.

Rather, the students were continually enjoined to freely express their thoughts. Disagreements among them often offered opportunities for gleaning insights into different aspects of life and living. This emphasis on the individual is evident in the *Analects*, in which Confucius engages with a wide variety of individual students, at times, highlighting a particularly good student as a model for the others, and urging them on, while at other times, gently admonishing them.

In all cases, however, Confucius showed respect for their rights to choose whichever path they wanted to pursue in life, and above all, to appreciate the value of each life. As Confucius notes, "When going abroad, treat everyone as if you were receiving a great guest. What you do not want for yourself, do not do to others" (Confucius 12:2). The individuality of the students was not denied by the teachings of the master, and everyone that they encountered on their life's journey should be seen as deserving of their utmost consideration and kindness just as they would expect from others. Because, every individual is important.

Confucianism recognized, however, that unfettered individualism was a potential recipe for disaster. As the philosopher, Gao, explains, disaster would ensue if everyone sought to exercise their passions (487). For example, the material goods of the world would not be enough if everyone decided to indulge in what they truly desired. For this reason, the ancient kings are said to have brought in not only rules and regulations but also rituals and moral principles that would govern the differences among the population, with the result that this "caused men to perform the duties of their status in life and each to receive his due" (491).

Even in the West, in societies such as the United States, where individualism is said to be the hallmark of the culture, for centuries, groups have gathered in churches, sports stadiums, and political communities either to refresh themselves or to appreciate anew the value of maintaining connections with others in their community. When it comes to the religious side, O'Brien maintains that even though many Americans succumb to religious authority and behavior in their lives, their participation is framed as voluntaristic, and therefore, individualistic (175). There is no reason why we cannot use the same logic to say that the Confucianists' participation in community rituals is likewise a matter of choice.

The emphasis on Confucian China as a communitarian society may be overstated. This is because cultural anthropologists suggest that no society is wholly one of holism or individualism; rather, every society trains its members to develop elements of both dependence and independence. Dependence training, for example, manifests in the form of "obedience to authority, developing a well-rounded personality, or fulfilling role duties" (Lim et al. 26).

Whether in ancient times or more recently, Confucian society has, like other societies, been complex. So, one might expect that any attempt to understand such societies will mean taking note of subtleties and nuances or even contradictions in the society.

In fact, according to Brindley, individualism did indeed develop in early China in connection with the sociopolitical events of that era. More pointedly, when individualism is understood through the prism of agency, Brindley draws a distinction between conformist agency and individual agency where the former refers to an individual who is merely the conduit to the exercise of authority and the latter, the actual source of authority (xxx). Brindley points out that in early China, individual agency was much more operative in society. Those identified with the notion of individual agency had the qualities that made them "capable of exerting agency from within a web of human, social, and cosmic relationships" (xxx). In this case, the person was autonomous, and used their judgment and initiative to do what needed to be done. On the other hand, those with conformist agency were seen as agents that would carry out an act because they had been given the authority by someone else.

William J. De Bary points out that from the very earliest periods of Chinese culture and philosophy, the issue of the individual has been ever-present (Learning for One's Self 2), and that the narrative of an oppressive system in which individuality was entirely subordinated to family and state in China does not hold. Rather, it seems to have been a story concocted by Western scholars who were not well versed in the literature and history of China and Confucianism. Individualism was not only present at the elite level of the culture but also the grassroots.

At the elite levels, the notion of individuality was "represented as the admiration of the independent personality of individual intellectuals" (Keqian 446). And at the grassroots level, it was represented in terms of how individuals were able to survive by their wits. This is exemplified in the following saying: "If one does not consider and do things for oneself, the person will be destroyed by Heaven and Earth" (446). Thus, both at the upper echelons of society and the lower levels, individuals sought to chart their path and were able to do so either through the power of their intellect or the power of their personality or skill.

Brindley's recognition of two different kinds of agency and the identification of individual agency as the primary form associated with Confucianism asserts that the individual's future was not foreordained, and that, to some extent, how individuals conducted themselves laid the foundation for how far they could go in life. Such an example is presented in the life of Shun of Yu, a humble man, whose father was blind, mother apparently deceitful, and brother Xiang, arrogant, but whose self-control and ability to live harmoniously with his family made him attractive enough to the emperor for Shun of Yu to be elevated to a leadership position in the realm (De Bary and Bloom, Sources of Chinese Tradition 30). In contrast to the upright but humble Shun of Yu, other individuals, who exerted themselves in intellectual pursuits and displayed similarly exquisite forms of character took a more conventional route to the top. Thus, the example of Shun of Yu shows that there was not a singular path to "greatness" and that family background was not a barrier to accessing opportunity and honor.

In fact, one of the most celebrated Confucian scholars, Ma Rong (AD 79-166), said quite plainly: "The individual life of man is indeed more cherishable than the entire world" (Munro, Individualism and Holism 125). This is a strong affirmation of the importance of an individual's place within the society. Among Confucianists, there was a continual quest for what was most authentic in an individual and the recognition that the individual had some powers that need not always be papered over by "false modesty or hypocrisy" (126).

Towards the end of the Han Dynasty, when Confucianism was in full flower, individuality had taken on a positive aspect, in contrast to sameness, which was said to be despised (126). This may not be so surprising in that as more and more people immersed themselves in the classics and disputed with one another regarding what was true and what was not, they must have become keenly aware of the growing strength of their convictions, the differences in their patterns of thinking and reasoning, and thus, a greater appreciation for their uniqueness and power. Even so, the best of Confucian practitioners held their egotism in check.

The next section considers how individuality in Confucianism also means that every individual is worthy of respect, and capable of developing their talents to the full.

# Notes

# CHAPTER 4
# INDIVIDUALISM IN RECOGNITION OF THE EQUAL WORTH OF ALL HUMAN BEINGS

Besides the easily understandable notion of individualism that places great emphasis on personal pursuits, individualism can also be seen from the point of view of how society views each member, and with that, the opportunities that are open to them. A society in which no arbitrary limits are placed on individuals at the point of birth could be seen as one that has a measure of respect for individuality. In this regard, Confucianism passes the test of upholding individualism. But, perhaps, one of the paradoxes of individualism is the recognition that, it "might lead to either an appreciation of human equality or a preoccupation with the inequality of man" (Béteille et al. 121). The idea of individualism is a complicated one.

This chapter focuses on how individualism can be

reflected in equality of opportunity; the next chapter shows how differences in effort exerted by different people can also show up as reflections of their individuality. In effect, respect for individualism can exist where society erects no barriers to the opportunities available to all at the outset of life. But then, a society that forces all its citizens to move in lockstep and restrains personal ambition would not be showing respect for individuality.

Confucianism taught that every child had the potential to rise to eminence through study and practice. In fact, "Confucius believed in human educability and carried out his own teaching without class discrimination" (Confucius 15:38; Hu, "Confucianism and Contemporary Chinese politics" 147). Confucius was a tireless pursuer of knowledge and wisdom, and he encouraged his followers to do the same; the goal was not just for them to distinguish themselves in the eyes of society. The central idea was that such self-cultivation, while useful as an end in itself, also served the purpose of making the individuals following this path worthy contributors to harmony within their homes, their communities, and the wider world. Although Confucianism was not, throughout its history, perfect in every sense, it attempted over the centuries to draw people towards the notion of virtue, without which no worldly attainment can gain genuine respect.

The Confucian civil service examination, which began in the early 600s (CE) in the Sui dynasty (Rainey 148) allowed people from different walks of life to become worthy contributors to their society based not just on the kind of family they had been born into but on their intellectual ability, commitment, persistence, and appreciation of morality. This commitment to education, which has continued to be upheld in many Confucian-influenced countries such as China, the two Koreas, and Japan, has indeed helped these societies to rise economically. It is with this in mind that Chinese-born American philosopher, Tu Weiming, in *Way, Learning, and Politics*, asserts that, "the great strength of modern East Asia is its intellectual and spiritual self-definition as a learning civilization. This may very well be the most precious legacy of Confucian humanism" (334). For Confucianists, the focus on canonical texts was the basis for inclusion in the Confucian family, but some scholars pointed out that it was not enough to read and memorize the texts and that action and application were paramount (Berthrong and Berthrong 56). It took years to memorize the texts, but the point was not mere memorization but for one to observe in one's own life how to apply the principles that had been absorbed through patient and endless repetition.

That Confucians saw human worth as being equal is found, for example, in the following statement by

Mencius: "How should I be different from others? Yao and Shun were the same as other men" (Eno "Mencius" 4B:32). Yao and Shun were held up as paragons of leadership and virtue and yet, they were not seen as superior to any other person. The Confucian endorsement of equality of opportunity, in particular, educational opportunity, is further confirmed in the following saying: "By nature close together [or alike, or the same], through practice set apart" (Confucius 17:2). This same idea is expressed, perhaps much more clearly in another translation, as follows: "By nature, men are nearly alike; through practice, they move apart" (Huang et al. 113). This recognizes that even though the starting point for all human beings might be the same, individuals play a part in whether they would remain at the basic level from where all human beings begin at birth, or if, through patient practice and effort, they would elevate themselves into models of good conduct and become worthy of emulation. And it should not be surprising that not all human beings are willing to go the distance in aiming towards becoming a *junzi* (a noble person). The road is hard and requires the kind of uncommon self-sacrifice that, not all individuals, for varying reasons, both personal and otherwise, would want to pursue.

Nevertheless, it is a road that is open to all (Munro, The Concept of Man 2), and thus, affirms that Confucian society recognizes the equal worth of all in the society.

As we shall see in the following chapter, however, it is for the same reason of showing respect for human individuality that those who seek to excel are given the opportunity in Confucian society to do so, even if it means surpassing their fellow human beings in the respect and regard that they are eventually accorded in the society.

## *Notes*

# CHAPTER 5
# INDIVIDUALISM AND THE HARD ROAD TOWARDS SELF-CULTIVATION

Though the idea of individualism being discussed in this book is in its positive sense, Uichol Kim, a researcher in indigenous, organizational, and child psychology, reminds us that individualism could also manifest as hedonism and egocentrism, which Confucianism condemns (Kim et al., Individualism and Collectivism 47). But there is also the individualism that tends towards self-fulfillment, which in Confucian society, is not just for the individual's self-gratification. Rather, this form of individualism allows for achieving personal goals while harnessing the benefits of those goals for the good of the community (48). It is also for this reason that in communitarian societies such as Confucian China, infighting among children within the family, whether close family members or the extended family or even neighbors, is frowned upon (48). From a very early age, children are taught that they are to be one another's keeper, especially if they are in the same family.

Confucianism makes a distinction between the masses (*min*) and the so-called superior or noble people (*junzi*) (Nuyen, "Confucianism and the Idea of Citizenship" 130), which makes it appear that those at the upper rungs of society have more rights. But the fact that those at the upper rungs of society have more options and opportunities is not in itself proof that Confucianism has no respect for the equal value of individuals. It just means that by dint of their greater level of education and understanding of the society, including the value of the goods that they can contribute, those at the upper rungs are perceived to be more deserving of respect. But such respect is not accorded because the *junzi* are seen as being intrinsically worth more than others.

The according of greater respect or power to some individuals cannot be presented as proof that the society has no respect for individuality. Nuyen argues that in the same way police officers might be accorded greater power in modern society, in Confucian society, people in different roles had access to varying levels of power. What is important, therefore, is whether Confucianism provides equality of opportunity in gaining such access to power. And there is no question that such an opportunity existed: "we can say that Confucians explicitly endorse equality of opportunities, particularly educational opportunity" (131). Jobs in the public sector were accorded based on the open and fair administration of examinations, meaning that, a person from the lower rungs of society who was sufficiently ambitious could gain access to the levers of power.

While acknowledging that self-cultivation is very much a part of Confucian culture, Ho asserts that in the Confucian warning to always stick to propriety, self-cultivation "should be differentiated from the notions of self-actualization held by humanistic psychologists in the West" (118). Ho explains further that the Confucian self is a subdued self, one "forced" to restrain the self. Actually, the restraint that Confucianism expresses is one of restraint from doing what is wrong. For example, if one had an impulse to hit someone that had annoyed them, the Confucian caution for restraint would be useful to remember.

The reason Confucianism could not have sought to dim anyone's lights and suppress talent is that the very purpose of Confucian dedication and education was for those who excelled to be in a position where they could walk with kings and queens and offer their advice. Thus, they were fully meant to become self-actualized human beings as far as their talents and efforts would take them.

The path to becoming a sage was a difficult one; the

successful student had to rely on the guidance of a teacher while at the same time demonstrating commitment to what would be a lifetime of personal devotion. Confucius, as a teacher, did not spoon-feed students and try to mold them in his image. He expected each individual to make an effort and to show some excitement about what they were learning. Moreover, Confucius did not expect that all who came to learn from him would be the same (Confucius 7.08).

In essence, in a world of meager resources and the need for hard work to survive, there had to be a good reason for which individuals would spend so much time at the feet of a master. For boys or men from poor families, education was the great leveler, and in a society where men of talent could rise as far as the court of the emperor, the sacrifices that such tutelage entailed could have been seen to be worth it. Even though the possibility of attaining a high position in society, and with it, material gain, were potential benefits for those who distinguished themselves as scholars, for Confucius himself, virtue was the goal. Tan acknowledges that while individual effort and a commitment to self-development were necessary to achieving greatness, the desired outcome spelled out in *The Great Learning* (*Daxue*) was not material accumulation and competition but rather "moral cultivation and collaboration" (Tan, Confucian Philosophy 10). The amount of effort and persistence required, however, suggests that individuals needed to be highly committed if they were to remain on the straight and narrow path towards moral growth.

In the *Doctrine of the Mean*, we learn that the biggest challenge of following the *Dao*, or the Way, does not lie just in its study but that it takes incredible effort to stay on the path. Giving up at any point of one's quest means that one has lost the race. Confucius said, "If I stop even one basketful of earth short of completion, then I have failed completely" (Confucius 9.19). Of the quest to become a person accomplished enough to be a role model, it is said: "Its secret does not lie in 'strange acts'; it lies in finding the persistence to walk it forever: to be 'centered' in ordinary practice until death" (Eno 23).

Lest one get the impression that only the *junzi* walked the path of the *Dao*, *The Doctrine of the Mean* points out that "the common farmer and his wife practice the Dao without knowing it" (23-24). The difficulty of staying on the path is highlighted still more when Confucius says that of the four key ways to the *Dao* of the *junzi*, he was unable to fulfill any of them: "To serve my father with that which I seek from my son—I cannot do it! To serve my ruler with that which I seek from my subordinates—I cannot do it! To serve my elders with that which I seek from my juniors—I cannot do it! To first practice towards my friend what I seek from them—

I cannot do it!" (28). Knowing that even Confucius himself had difficulty living up to these ideals humanizes the process of striving, making all other strivers after the virtuous life recognize that they are not deficient if they are struggling with some aspects. For, after all, Confucius himself had his difficulties; but then again, having difficulties is no reason to quit trying.

In a society lacking respect for individualism, consanguinity, that is, relationship to an ancestor, might, for example, have been the sole basis for selecting leaders. But Confucian society recognized that each individual had the power of choice to determine the course of their lives and there was ample freedom for people to so choose if they were willing to make the necessary sacrifices. It was, to some extent, a matter of individual ambition whether one chose to be a farmer or a scholar. And the society was ready to give its glory to those who had done the hard work of preparing themselves for those honors.

Self-cultivation, also, was not something that one accomplished solely on one's own. Rather, it involved learning directly or indirectly from others, but always with the individual at the center. As Confucius stated, "When walking with two other people, I will always find a teacher among them. I focus on those who are good and seek to emulate them, and those who are bad remind me what needs to be changed" (Confucius 7.22).

In this Confucian comment is seen the value that the master placed on each person irrespective of the level of accomplishment of that person. Also, as Confucius said, "Study as though you can't catch up to it, as though you fear to lose it" (Confucius 8.17). This recognizes the incessant effort required to master a subject.

Over the years, accomplished individuals sought to make the path of learning a little easier for those who would come after them. Knowledgeable individuals sought to share their experiences with others or provide some guidance that others could follow. One such effort was undertaken by Zhu Xi (Chu Hsi), who divided *The Great Learning* into two, with a brief earlier section and a latter longer section comprising commentary. This structure has become widely accepted, with the text portion introducing eleven central themes and the commentary section enlarging upon them. *The Great Learning* lays out the progression from being an ordinary human being to the level of sagehood, a process that is said to comprise eight stages of practice, namely, 1) aligning affairs, 2) extending understanding, 3) making intentions germane, 4) balancing the mind, 5) refining one's person, 6) aligning one's household, 7) ordering the state, and 8) setting the world at peace. These stages are governed by the following three principles: a) Making one's "bright virtue" brilliant, b) making the people new, and c) coming to rest in the highest good.

It is clear from the above that the learning journey is nothing to take lightly. It is mostly for those who have a strong streak of willpower to go the distance.

The first five of the eight elements focus on what an individual can do. It is not about rushing out to change the world but to first look inward, not in an egoistic way, but to weed out of one's personality anything that would make one unfit to be an upstanding member of the community. Even though the individual is encouraged to look inward, the ultimate advice is not for people to seek to enrich themselves, but to make the world a better place.

Regarding the systematic process of personal growth, we read in *The Great Learning*,

In ancient times, those who wished to make bright virtue brilliant in the world first ordered their states; those who wished to align their household first refined their persons; those who wished to refine their persons first balanced their mind; those who wished to balance their minds first perfected the genuineness of their intentions; those who wished to perfect the genuineness of their intentions first extended their understanding; extending one's understanding lies in aligning affairs. (Eno 11)

A person who takes to heart the words of Confucius and the teachings of the *Great Learning* is apt to study more frequently to keep the material fresh in their mind and to reinforce through practice what has been learned. But, as important as books are to the project of self-cultivation, more was called for; character development was a central pillar, along with other skills such as archery, music, building, and management. All of these practices were not simply for the sheer joy that they could bring; rather, they allowed practitioners to cultivate persistence and appreciate the steady progress of development over time (Confucius 5.15). In learning to master any skill, one moves ahead in fits and starts. The faint of heart gives up. Whereas those who are truly determined can realize, eventually, the joy of being masters at their craft. These artistic endeavors, therefore, serve also as metaphors for the journey of becoming a *ren*, that is, cultivating the spirit of humanity or humaneness.

The teachings of Confucius included the mastery of rituals and the kind of self-cultivation that would help the learners become masters of themselves. The virtues towards which disciples had to strive included the following, all of which center on individual agency and consideration for other individuals: benevolence/humaneness (*ren*); filial piety (*xiao*); rightness/appropriateness (*yi*); ritual propriety (*li*); loyalty (*zhong*); self-reflection (*shu*); trustworthiness (*xin*); and wisdom (*zhi*). The effort towards the cultivation of each of the above required uncommon discipline and self-sacrifice, once again, pointing to the reality that people without a sense of personal or individual drive could not hope to make much headway. The tension was ever-present between individualism, which allows for trying things out and "experimenting without constraint" (Huggins and Thompson 123), and social harmony, which calls for loyalty and the exhibition of continual care for others.

Those who embark on the path of self-cultivation may aim at either becoming a "gentleman" or a "sage," with both cases requiring the incessant practice of virtue, but being a sage is at a significantly higher level than being a "gentleman." The training to become either one of these is serious and requires the individual to undergo stringent traditional practice that involves both study and ritual practice. Because of the amount of commitment it takes over a long period and requiring as it does the mastery of a wide range of skills and understanding of copious amounts of texts, a person without a strong sense of individualism would probably not be able to follow through with it.

The effort to master rituals, which were seen as part of the civilizing process, were "voluntaristic in nature and not coercive" (De Bary, Asian Values and Human Rights 13). They were not the kinds of practices that were enforced by the state and subject to the pain of incarceration or death if one were unable to follow it to the letter. But it required time and attention to detail. As

Slingerland explains, "after extended training in these practices, the emotions are ultimately harnessed to produce moral behavior, which springs spontaneously from personal inclination" ("Virtue Ethics" 101). It is also not just a matter of sitting at the feet of the master to be lectured to. On the other hand, it involves willingness on the part of the individual to think and practice what they are learning. The mental and emotional investment required on the part of the student can be inferred from the following comment by Confucius in the *Analects*:

I will not enlighten a heart that is not already struggling to understand, nor will I provide the proper words to a tongue that is not already struggling to speak. If I hold up one corner of a problem and the student cannot come back to me with the other three, I will not attempt to instruct him again. (Confucius 7.8)

Confucian training recognizes that the best way to build people up and help them to become independent is not to do everything for them but to let them take some responsibility for their growth. While we see the necessity for interaction between teacher and student, it is not done in a way that paralyzes the student and makes them perpetually dependent on the teacher. A person who learns the necessity of personal effort, coupled with guidance from someone more knowledgeable, is likely to know what it means to be of service to others.

Confucian training was not easy. It required consistency and constancy over a lifetime. This is exemplified in the life of Confucius when towards the end, he could speak with a measure of satisfaction that he had made some progress. As he says, "At age fifteen I set my heart upon learning, at thirty, I took my stand; at forty I became free of doubts; at fifty I understood the Heavenly mandate; at sixty my ear was attuned; and at seventy I could follow my heart's desire without overstepping the bounds of propriety" (Confucius 2.4; Slingerland 114). The phrase, "I set myself upon" clearly shows that it was an individual decision to pursue the path of learning and wisdom. Having lost his father as a young boy and his mother while in his teens, he was in "impoverished and unfortunate" (Weiming and Ikeda 89) straits. He could have easily lost his way. But even at that young age, he had the determination to choose a path for himself and was able to persist on this path so that by thirty he was sure that the decision had been a correct one.

Weiming and Ikeda note that Confucius was also not unaware that he had to teach by example and that the dedication he applied to "a wide variety of subjects in depth" (89) helped him to develop "internal strength" (89). Though the path he set for formal education came to predominate in China for almost two and a half millennia, in his youth, he worked at several menial jobs, but he never lost sight of the goal that he had set for himself to attain a senior government position (Schuman

11). Even after choosing a path of learning, the scholar who sought to live a life of morality was beset by innumerable temptations in a world of factions and conflicts. This meant that the individual had to make important decisions, take principled stands, and hold back from being swept up in greed and ambition. While Confucius himself was able to stand this test, for centuries, many Confucian scholars fell prey to ambition and were not unwilling to "sacrifice their beliefs" (11) to curry favor with whichever emperor they were courting. Schuman points out that Confucius was far from perfect and that he not only doubted his abilities at times but that he also sometimes "came across as arrogant" (11). He was not afraid of debating with others, a practice that indicates that both within Confucianism and the wider world of Chinese society, people were free to express their points of view and to fight passionately for their positions.

The next chapter explains the habits of mind that the *junzi* had to cultivate. In addition to the mastery of rituals and the development of a sense of propriety in dealing with various responsibilities in the society, they needed to develop the strength of character to push back on the powerful. In other words, they carried their moral mantle with strength and pride.

*Notes*

# CHAPTER 6

# BECOMING A PERSON OF VIRTUE: LEARNING TO STAND ALONE

It is a mistake to assume that the attempt to create social harmony meant kowtowing to every kind of social or political pressure. On the contrary, the voluntary decision to embark on a life of virtue meant learning to stand alone, to not, for example, condone corruption. Those who sought to cultivate themselves as strong moral agents and models in the society could not succeed if they were weak beings that could easily be trampled upon. On the other hand, they had to be willing to boldly criticize others, including kings and princes "who failed to live up to their moral standards" (O'Dwyer). To develop such a strong backbone, to be both fearless critics and worthy role models, they needed to cultivate a wide range of virtues over a long period.

## Benevolence/Humaneness (*ren*)

In looking at the Chinese characters that make up the word, humaneness (仁), one observes one part with the symbol of a person (人), and the other, the number 'two' (二). This has been taken by some commentators to signify the feeling of compassion that exists between two human beings (Yushun 119). Those who are described as *ren* are not the ordinary run of people. Rather, they are people who have learned to so comport themselves, both in word and deed, that they cut a particularly striking picture (Littlejohn 29). This is because such a person is expected to have undergone and endured hardship and also known what it means to enjoy happy circumstances (Confucius 4.2). Such people are also expected to have the discernment of being able to identify other good people and to have expunged as much as is possible the desire to do wrong. They are always ready to part from those who are determined to go astray (4.7). So highly did Confucius think of people with humaneness that he proclaimed that the best possible place for a person to live is a community in which there was *ren* (4.1). It is interesting that, despite Confucius's praise for *ren*, he resisted identifying any of his contemporaries, including himself, as the kind of *ren* that others should follow.

Rather, he left the possibility open that no matter how much one might have striven to follow in the *Dao*, the Way, there was always room to grow. The *Dao*, as Brindley explains, is variously conceived of as a cosmic authority or universal force that is unrestricted to all but attainable through study and practice, the path to being a sage (32). Confucius praised one of his disciples, Yan Hui, for being able to embrace the mindset of *ren* for months whereas others only clung to it perfunctorily. Of this Yan Hui, Confucius said, "Yan Hui was content with only a bowl of rice, a gourd of water and a small place to live!" (Analects 6.11). This is a reminder of the hard road that those in pursuit of life on the morally correct track had to follow. They were to avoid temptations such as bribes or the easy road that might have meant caring more about themselves than other equally valuable human beings. Whether one would resist such temptations or remain steadfast was not a decision that any community could take for an individual. Rather, it required personal conviction in the teachings that one had imbibed, and it required personal fortitude in being able to say no to what was unethical or improper. Sadly, not all Confucianists passed this moral test.

Confucius looked upon the Zhou dynasty (1046-256 BCE) as an era when the practice of rectitude had reached its greatest height. Thus, the words of the Odes and other classics from that era furnished a good base of knowledge for Confucius and his followers to not only ponder over but to live and explore every day. As Yu reports, the classics of ancient history that existed in Confucius's time were not in good condition. Confucius undertook the arduous task of systematically investigating the traditional texts by collecting, studying, editing, and then using them to create a "literary curriculum of his own school" (179). Confucius saw himself, then, not as an innovator, but as someone who was trying to remain faithful to some of the traditions of the past. Through studying and thinking, and applying the teachings to the needs of his time, he was able to introduce innovations and to inspire the love of learning in a great many people.

While the original meaning of *junzi* was about a person of noble birth (Slingerland 111), Confucius believed that anyone who demonstrated sufficient will and rectitude ought to be given the chance to study and to do so "without regard to the person's social background or status" (111). In essence, the right heart attitude was more important than being of noble birth. Individuals' attitude towards learning, coupled with how they comported themselves, could very well determine the heights to which they could attain.

The word *ren* has variously been interpreted as benevolence, humaneness, goodness, and a host of others. Yu maintains that since the words "humanity" or "humaneness" relate more to the innate characteristics of a person, it does not properly reflect the meaning of *ren*, observing that *ren* is a "cultivated disposition" (179). As such, rather than the use of humanity or humaneness, Yu suggests the use of "human excellence" (179). People who have trained themselves to manifest what is truly human might be called *ren*. It must be understood that *ren* is not a matter of one's natural inborn qualities but the manifestation of years of effort in an individual's constant attempt to live a life of rectitude. At its core, *ren* "involves an altruistic concern for others and would reflect the tender aspect of human feelings" (Li, The sage and the second sex 25). As Li writes of this self-regulation, it is "refined and developed through the interactions involved in...relationships" (Woods and Lamond 673).

Thus, more than the Hippocratic oath to do no harm, *ren* also suggests showing empathy to people. It is not about isolating oneself but being involved in the world and caring about those around. It is virtually impossible to develop *ren* in isolation from others. The practice of *ren* presupposes action concerning many different kinds of people. This means assuming a role within a community of other practitioners while learning under the instruction of a teacher and ensuring that one's individuality, in terms of agency and the will to persist, remained intact.

Even though the idea of self-cultivation makes it seem as though the individual stands completely alone,

Confucius makes it crystal clear that this is not necessarily the case. Confucius said, "I once spent an entire day without food and an entire evening without sleep—engaged in thought. It did not benefit me at all. It is better to study" (Confucius 15.30). Rather than just mulling things over by oneself, studying gives you the foundation upon which to engage with others, that is, to commune with the great minds of the past.

The students, individuals though they may be, from the very beginning, are reminded of their connection to others. The student learns to appreciate the kernel of wisdom in Confucius's thinking, that no person stands alone, and that, when it comes to knowledge, it is preferable to seek the counsel of wiser heads, through the reading of appropriate ancient texts and discourse. The two elements, study and practice, are wedded together, prompting the exclamation, "Is it not a joy to study and then to practice what one has learned!" (1.1). And what is practice but the expression of what one has learned in the company of one's fellow human beings?

In the Western philosophical tradition, the idea of a person presupposes an independent entity that has "moral and political rights" (Bockover 317). This idea has persisted through the centuries, with many associated with the West often concerned about how to preserve such independence and individuality. The Confucian self, however, is not a separate entity. Rather, it is one that is "inescapably interdependent with other persons and is never conceived as independent even when 'individual' qualities unique to a person can be identified (317). It should not be forgotten that the opportunity to cultivate individual qualities did not mean deliberately severing ties with the society. In effect, for Confucians, it was not necessary to be a hermit to be able to have self-direction or a sense of individual purpose. Isolation was not synonymous with individuality.

It was also not the case that becoming *ren* meant that one necessarily had to be in government service. When Confucius was questioned about why he did not have a position with the government, he responded: "It is all in filial conduct (*xiao*)! Just being filial to your parents and befriending your brothers is carrying out the work of government" (Confucius 2.21). This recognizes that how one behaves towards the family and other people around has an impact on the prevailing atmosphere in the land. If every family could do its part in the sense of fostering harmony, it would redound into a country that was living in harmony.

Another way in which goodness spreads is when exemplary persons (*junzi*) sincerely commit to their parents. The people around them, observing their wonderful example, would quite likely make an effort to express their own sense of humaneness (*ren*). They will show care and consideration towards one another. According to Confucius, the excellence of the "exemplary person (*junzi*) is the wind, while that of the petty person is the grass. As the wind blows, the grass is sure to bend" (12.9). This effect that the *junzi* has on people does not depend on their being in government service. If each *junzi* could make the people in their immediate circle a little more concerned about morality, the ripples of goodness could spread across the land. Perhaps, there is no more powerful statement of the importance of the individual than the assertion in the *Analects* that one wise person, living a righteous life, could help change society for the better.

## Desire

One committed to the path of *ren* (humaneness/benevolence) could not continue to live within their animal nature, that is, one in which desires are unrestrained. Mencius writes that "in cultivating one's heart-mind, nothing is more effective than having few desires" (Eno "Mencius" 7B:35). This is because a person that is full of desires could not maintain the unswerving sense of rectitude needed to be a sage, the highest stage of *ren*. Rather, desire has to be controlled so that it does not cross into the territory of greed. This injunction is not made to a community. It is made to a person since Mencius recognizes that each individual has to decide whether to go through the strictures and moral restraint that the path of morality requires. Greedy people want to have more for themselves so that others might have less. Such people are, therefore, only concerned with their own well-being.

Confucius was even willing to make a connection between excessive desires and crime, which destabilizes a society. When Ji Kangzi expressed concern about growing criminality in Lu and sought advice from Confucius about how to handle this problem, Confucius responded that "If you could just get rid of your own excessive desires, the people would not steal even if you rewarded them for it" (Confucius 12:18).

Confucius focuses on what an individual can do. Confucius draws attention to how the greed and conspicuous consumption of even one individual could have a detrimental effect on society. Confucius highlights the specter of envy and jealousy among those who are unable to afford what the 'rich' have. Rather than blaming the criminals, Confucius seemed to believe that those individuals who made a show of their wealth were not showing enough care and concern for others, and that, with their desire to accumulate material things and to show them off, they were inadvertently contributing to possible instability in society.

It also seems that those who make the pursuit of wealth their sole goal are not seen as caring enough about their fellow human beings. This, of course, would apply to those who simply want to accumulate wealth for its own sake. For this reason, the person who is dedicated to following the *Dao*, or the Way, would not make the pursuit of wealth the only goal. As Confucius stated, "If wealth were an acceptable goal, even though I would have to serve as a groom holding a whip in the marketplace, I would gladly do it" (7.12). Of course, because the singular pursuit of wealth is not seen as an acceptable goal, one is unlikely to see Confucius with any such whip in hand. It is also a not-so-subtle message that people should not be willing to do just about anything in the pursuit of wealth. So those on this magnificent quest for *ren* put themselves in a position where they can follow their heart's desire without necessarily overstepping the bounds. They cannot intentially do the wrong thing and make excuses as though they had no serious acquaintance with the tenets and principles of the *Dao*.

Confucianism encouraged the suppression of desires, but this does not mean that Confucianism did not care about the individual and their happiness or rights. In fairness, Confucius did not focus on individual human rights as we have come to expect in modern society. His was a ritual-governed society rather than one based on the law. Confucius believed that the state was somewhat of a larger version of the family. In fact,

> Far from individuals requiring protection from a powerful state or others in the community, early Confucians believed that the rulers were their protectors and

other individuals were like their family members. Under such an arrangement, there is no need for empowering individuals with rights to participate in politics to ensure the rulers' justice or to ensure peaceful relations with others. (Sim 6)

Striving to get to the point of *ren* is not just beneficial for the individual concerned. Confucius asserts that it is even more important than water and fire, two elements that are important for everyday functioning. But these two elements can both kill, useful as they are. Confucius reminds those with whom he is conversing that, he has "yet to see a casualty from humaneness" (15.35).

In one sense then, it might be said that family forms the bedrock, the root, and the foundation of *ren* because it is within one's own family where one gets the most frequent opportunities to put into practice the elements of *ren*.

Confucius explains quite clearly what is involved in the difficult journey of becoming a gentleman. He says that "When native substance overwhelms cultural refinement, the result is a crude rustic. When cultural refinement overwhelms native substance, the result is a foppish pedant. Only when culture and native substance are perfectly mixed and balanced do you have a gentleman" (6.18). To this, Slingerland observes that becoming a gentleman, thus, requires striking the right balance between social forms: on the one hand, performance of the rites and study, and on the other, individual participation involving the emotions and intellectual curiosity ("Virtue Ethics" 102).

Book learning should not be divorced from the everyday life experiences of the people. Those who isolate themselves and have their heads always buried in books are likely to lose the common sense that is necessary to deal with many aspects of life. They might lose the common touch. The gentleman is not given prescriptions to apply to situations but rather timeless principles upon which sound judgment can be based. Living by principles shows confidence in the individual's ability, over time, to make sensible decisions rather than being led about and pushed around as though mindless. It is for this reason that Confucius says, "Acting in the world, the gentleman has no predispositions for or against anything" (4.10). He has to consider the situation and apply his thinking faculties that have been honed through study and experience. In the treatment of his disciples, Confucius did not apply the same yardstick. Rather, he took account of their different personalities. Confucius handled individuals differently: "Zan Yu is retiring and slow, therefore I urge him forward. Chi Lu has more than his share of energy, therefore I keep him back" (11:21). With this, Confucius indicates that human beings are not all the same, even if they are equal. There is an acknowledgment in Confucianism that particular situations call for site-specific-person-centered responses. In one's interactions, applying one formula to every situation is apt to bring about bad results in some cases, and so, being prepared to act at any moment, with consideration for the particular facts of each case, is what matters.

Another situation that shows that Confucianism was not just a matter of blindly following rules is found in the statement about Confucius in the *Analects*: "When receiving a gift from a friend—even something as valuable as a cart or a horse—he did not bow unless it was a gift of sacrificial meat" (10:23). There is no clause in the books on rites declaring whether a friend should be thanked for a gift. Confucius, knowing the special place that sacrificial meat held in the rites, was able to make the judgment himself that for anything other than that, it was not necessary to make a bow. It may also be that Confucius did not want to become beholden to friends who may be using gifts to ingratiate themselves, and so, by not bowing, he took a neutral attitude toward it.

**Timeliness**

One of the characteristics for which Confucius was renowned among his disciples and in his life was his recognition of the importance of time, that is, when to take action and when not to. In this regard, it was not a matter of following rules but paying attention to the facts and conditions of the moment, and then making the right decision. As Mencius reports,

"When Confucius decided to leave Qi, he emptied the rice from the pot before it was ever done and set out immediately. When he decided to leave Lu he said, "I will take my time, for this is the way to leave the state of one's parents" (Eno "Mencius" 5B.1). Timeliness requires perpetual focus; for a person to be consistently timely in their dealings, they have to be attentive, both to self and the environment.

Whether in dealing courteously with others, showing consideration for members of one's family, or even participating in public affairs, one has to pay careful attention so as not to take action out of proper season. This would also include communication with others, as words said at the wrong time might have an unintended or even negative effect. It is with this in mind that Cheng notes that, "Timeliness is thus simply the comportment of a person, his faculty and action according to the individual situation" (The Primary Way 375). As a teacher who imparted knowledge by both precept and action, Confucius's comment that "Qiu is timid, therefore I encourage him; You is aggressive, therefore I restrain him" (Analects 11:22) is instructive along the same dimensions of knowing when to act and when not to. Confucius paid attention to both the little things and the truly important ones, meaning that he paid as much attention to when he ate (10.6) as to when he expressed himself (14:3). The foregoing strengthens the undercurrent of individualism in Confucianism; there was human agency, and timeliness. The individual needed to pay attention daily, but this was not beyond the capabilities of any serious person.

### Filial Piety (*xiao*)

In the Western world, there is the oft-quoted proverb, 'Charity begins at home.' Whether an individual will go out and have a positive effect on the world, in the Confucian ethos, is also rooted in what one learns and practices at home. Confucius says in the *Hsiao Ching*, "Now filial piety is the root of (all) virtue, and (the stem) out of which grows (all moral) teaching" (Taylor 47). This makes sense in that, if you show love, care, and consideration for your parents, you could be the kind of person who walks through the world with a sense of awareness about the importance of honoring people who have sacrificed for you. It would also mean that, for these parents that you care about, you will not do anything that will embroil them in disgrace or harm them in any way. Thus, consideration for one's parents has a benefit that redounds to the society at large. This idea is also encapsulated in the *Book of Poetry*, as follows: "Rising early and going to sleep late / Do not disgrace those who gave you birth" (Legge The Book of Poetry 335). And as if to drum the importance of filial piety deep into the consciousness of the people, Confucius further says in the *Hsiao Ching*, "Of all the actions of man there is none greater than filial piety" (Legge The Classic of Filial Piety 16).

Acquiring knowledge and status does not mean that the possessors of such have to lord it over others. Rather, part of becoming *ren* is to learn how to be discreet and respectful.

One of the best explanations of the importance of filial piety and how it can affect the larger society is given by Yuzi, one of Confucius's disciples, who suggests that a person who has grown up as a filial son or a respectful younger brother is likely to carry that feeling of respect to others. Such a person is likely to respect elderly people wherever the encounter occurs. As he continues, "The gentleman applies himself to the roots. Once the roots are firmly planted, the Way (*Dao*) will grow therefrom (Confucius 1.4, 1.6, 2.10). This applies to the person's dealings with others whether on a one-on-one basis or on a community-wide basis.

The observance of filial piety affords many opportunities by which a person can extend the sensitivity gained within the family to the outside world. The story is told of Zai Wo, who wondered aloud to Confucius why it was that the standard mourning period following the death of a father was as long as three years. He wondered if it could be shortened. Confucius assured him that if he wanted to shorten it, it was his choice.

We see here another instance of individual agency and responsibility rather than an imposition from on high the kind of personal decisions individuals ought to make. But then, after Zai Wo had left, Confucius remarked with some bitterness to his disciples: "How lacking in *ren* this Zai Wo is! A child is completely dependent upon the care of his parents for three years—this is why the three-year mourning period is a universal custom. Did not this Zai Wo receive three years of love from his parents?" (Slingerland 118). The bitterness that Confucius expresses is not unreasonable. Children are nurtured and protected for many years before they can stand on their own; acknowledging this by showing respect to one's parents in mourning seems fair. Even so, it is the kind of practice that one hopes will be done from a pure heart rather than done because of outside pressure. The individual who has grown in knowledge and wisdom ought to, at some point in life, make decisions that reflect this sense of maturity.

Confucius had a family of his own, including "a wife, daughter, and son" (Confucius 5.1, 11.8). The importance of family is cemented in the Chinese language, in that, one says not just "brother" but "elder brother or younger brother" (Knowles 19). Likewise, one says "older sister or younger sister" (Knowles 19). The need for young people to care for their parents is expressed in

Confucius's words: "While your parents are alive, you should not journey far afield; and if you travel, be sure to go to a specific destination" (4.19). This can also be seen as a check on the kind of individualism that is negative, that is, egoistic or self-centered. Confucius does not forbid anyone to travel since an individual has free will and can choose to do what they want. But individuals ought to be able to think of the consequences of their actions. People who care about their parents would not put themselves so out of reach that they end up living in regret if they are not able to properly respond to the needs of those parents in a moment of crisis.

The *Zhongyong*, quoting the *Classic of Poetry*, reflects on the idea of family relationships thus: "The loving relationship with wife and children, is like the strumming of the zither and the lute; in the harmony between the older and younger brothers, there is great joy and pleasure" (Lambert 154). Confucius promoted harmony in the family and the importance of obedience. But he also recognized that sometimes, parents themselves might be the problem. His advice, however, was that "In serving your parents you may gently dispute with them. But if it becomes clear you cannot change their opinions, you should resume an attitude of deference and not oppose them; even if discouraged, do not be resentful" (Confucius 4.18). It highlights wisdom that is expressed in more recent parlance in the expression,

"Do you want to be right or do you want to be happy?" Insisting on being right, in any relationship, often leads to much unfruitful discord. So, the wise person, sometimes, for the sake of peace and harmony, should not be averse to letting go of matters that are not so consequential. Asked explicitly about how to be *ren*, Confucius responded thus: "Be deferential in daily life, be respectful in handling affairs and be sincere in dealing with people" (13.9). From this we see, in yet another way, how important it was for the person on the path to cultivating *ren* to respect everyone, whether of high or low station.

### Ritual Propriety/Ritual (*li*)

Rituals may sound like unnecessary traditions today, but they do serve an important purpose. Confucius believed that when the gentleman (*junzi*), followed ritual propriety (*li*), this had an indirect effect on the common people, motivating and prompting them to attempt to behave with a sense of virtue. But these rites were not just robotic movements that practitioners had to go through. Rather, they required the practitioner's full attention. Rites covered a wide range, including meals, conversation, drinking, and clothing for different occasions. Besides, there were rites on gift-giving and even the correct posture while sleeping (Littlejohn 28). As the Master says, "If I am not fully present at the sacrifice, it is as if I did not sacrifice at all" (Confucius 3.12). In effect, practitioners learned to give fully of themselves to their roles. This could carry on into the individual practitioner's everyday life.

Mastering the rites involves learning rules and principles, but such knowledge is meant to fortify the person to the point where they can act on the spur of the moment. Besides, rituals are not meant to create a rigid, inflexible human being. Rather, "training ourselves in rituals means learning when and how to create or alter them" (Puett and Gross-Loh 50). It can be inferred from this that mere book learning was not enough for one to become a gentleman. Confucius said, "Imagine a person who can recite the three hundred Odes by heart but, when delegated a governmental task, is unable to carry it out or, when sent out into the field as a diplomat, is unable to use his own initiative—no matter how many Odes he might have memorized. What good are they to him?" (13.5)

Note the use of the phrase, "his own initiative" in the quotation above. The element of practical application, of individual agency based on a foundation of knowledge, is an important feature of these rituals, that is, learning to be a decisive person.

It seems that Confucius did not believe in doing things by halves. He did not believe in just going through the motions. As he said, "If I myself do not participate in the sacrifice, it is as though I have not sacrificed at all" (Littlejohn 37). But there were times when he was not directly involved, and yet, knew how to show the requisite respect. Thus, we read in the *Analects*: "When the villagers were performing the end-of-year exorcism (*nuo*), he (Confucius) would stand on the Eastern steps dressed in full court regalia" (Confucius 10.14). In Confucius's own life and his teachings, he sought to provide an example of good judgment, not dogmatic behavior.

The differences in human disposition also highlight the importance of rituals and how these can help different people acquire the right temperament that can lead them smoothly through life. As Confucius says, "If you are respectful but lack ritual training you will become exasperating; if you are careful but lack ritual training you will become timid; if you are courageous but lack ritual training, you will become unruly; and if you are upright, but lack ritual training, you will become inflexible." (8.2)

In all these cases, it is very clear that the bad outcome is not only to the individual's disadvantage but also that of others. For example, a person who is always exasperating to others is going to engender bad feelings, quarrels, or even fights that might endanger life and limb. Such an outcome in any society is unwelcome.

Likewise, a person who becomes too timid will not be of much use in those times that call for courage such as the need to fend off enemies or defend the home or the community. As in the first case, a person lacking ritual training but who allows their courageous attitude to bleed into unruliness will become a nuisance or worse to those around, hampering progress in any family, community, or societal efforts to advance. And finally, inflexibility has its dangers. There are times when a community has to shed old attitudes and embrace something new. But for those who cling to the past, this can be terrible for the progress of the community. So, rituals serve a variety of purposes on all the different temperaments and dispositions of those who have the benefit of Confucian training.

It must be noted that the *junzi* were not passive individuals. They were very much involved in life. As Tu explains, the ideal Confucian was someone who assumed many different roles in life. As scholar-officials, they shouldered political responsibilities and performed educational functions in society. Like Indian gurus, they were teachers; like Buddhist monks, they were ethical examples; like Jewish rabbis, they were learned scholars; like Greek philosophers, they were wise men; like Christian priests, they were spiritual leaders, and like Islamic mullahs, they were community leaders. (Tu, "Confucian Humanism in Perspective" 333)

Ritual propriety is not only about learning how to observe rituals and communicate with people at the higher echelons of society. Rather, it encompasses a whole range of a person's relationships. Confucius himself, as the exemplar for ritual propriety, is described as follows: "At court, in conversation with the lower ranks of grandees, he was familiar; in conversation with the upper ranks of grandees, he was respectful. When the ruler was present, he walked with a quick step, yet evenly" (Woods and Lamond 673). He could fit into any environment because he had taken the initiative to imbibe the knowledge and skills that made it possible for him to flexibly deal with the wide range of humanity that he came in contact with.

### Flexibility

One of the reasons Confucianism was able to endure for so many centuries is that it was flexible. It was not rigid even though there were well-articulated values towards which individuals were encouraged to strive towards. Confucianism acknowledged that the same judgment could not be applied to every single situation and that context had to be taken into consideration. Inflexibility, therefore, was seen as a negative. Confucius said, "A gentleman who studies is unlikely to be inflexible" (Confucius 1:8). Such a person, as one might expect, will have the wisdom to adapt to different environments without necessarily losing their moral core.

More evidence of flexibility is shown in the statement, "A cap made of hemp is prescribed by the rites, but nowadays people use silk. This is frugal, and I follow the majority. To bow before ascending the stairs is what is prescribed by the rites, but nowadays people bow after ascending" (15.11). Confucius, here, shows an understanding of what is important and what is not. If people are willing to be frugal in a matter that is not so important to the performance of rites, certainly, it might be excused. But this did not mean casting aside all the expectations about rites.

In another case, Zigong wondered why it was necessary to sacrifice a lamb at the appearance of the new moon. Confucius retorted: "Zigong! You regret the loss of the lamb; whereas I regret the loss of the rite" (3.17). There was indeed a need for flexibility but this did not mean turning the whole world of rites upside down and making up one's own rules. Knowing when to let go and when to hold fast was the mark of a person on the right path towards *ren*.

## Loyalty (*zhong*)

Beyond the family, friendship affords another opportunity for a gentleman to strengthen the bonds of community and to demonstrate loyalty. As with filial piety, a person who has learned the value of loyalty to friends and family is likely to extend this to the community at large and the society as a whole. It was in speaking about friendship that Confucius revealed what joy meant to him, that the desire to appreciate and to be appreciated by others is very much a natural part of life, and not only that but a welcome part of life.

It would be wrong, therefore, to assume that the strictures imposed by following the *Dao*, the Way, means that followers are without any form of joy in their lives. Confucius often remarked about his love of music. Not only that, he played the *Qin*, a zither-like instrument. He also liked to sing, as reported in the *Analects*. "When the Master sang with others and they sang well, he would always wait and then ask them to repeat before joining in harmony" (Confucius 7:32). While the performance might have been in a group, it was the coming together of individuals who had chosen to share and enjoy one another's company, that was of greater importance.

There was a time when Confucius was asked about his followers and their desires. After hearing all the different goals, Confucius said that he approved most of all the plans of Zeng Xi, the one who said that his wish was to go out in the company of friends at the end of spring, to bathe in the river, to revel in the cool breezes, and then return home singing.

This is a state of being in harmony with the self and the social and natural environment, although nothing in this state appears to be particularly "moral." (Ni 343)

It is also perhaps not an accident that Zeng Xi's idea

of fun included friends. Once again, this emphasizes the stamp of approval that the Master placed on building good, trusting relationships with people around, and in being able to choose for oneself what to delight in.

Confucius also said that one of the most joyous moments in life is "to have companions arrive from afar" (Confucius 1.1). Considering that Confucius dealt with adults as students rather than children, the kind of friendship he is talking about here possibly involves being in the company of people who share one's moral aspirations. This might be inferred from what Confucius says elsewhere that, "One should not befriend a person who is not as good as oneself" (1.8). This doesn't mean that those who are pursuing the Way are better than others. Rather, it is a simple recognition that bad friends can turn people away from following the path of rectitude. With good friends who are more or less on the same moral plane, a person can evaluate their progress and make adjustments where necessary. If such friends are all struggling to be better in a moral sense, then, it stands to reason that they can help one another, sharpen one another, as iron sharpens iron.

Loyalty springs from trust or trustworthiness (*xin*). A person who has allegiance to moral principles can be trusted to do the right thing at the right time. A person who has a record of truth-telling becomes a "dependable support for others" (Woods and Lamond 673). When it comes to trust, it is not a matter of what the community thinks. Rather, individuals have to cultivate their sensibilities. As Confucius said, "It is not the failure of others to appreciate your abilities that should trouble you, but rather your own lack of them" (Confucius 14:30). Individuals have to chart their course in life to develop both specific and general skills. This follow-through and care that is attached to one's commitments are not only towards one's superiors. As Zixia, a disciple of Confucius, said, "If a person treats worthy people as worthy and so alters his expression, exerts all his effort when serving his lord, and is trustworthy in keeping his word when in the company of friends, though others may say he is not learned, I would call him learned" (Woods and Lamond 673). This is further confirmation of what has been pointed out before, that, Confucianism demands consideration for people from all stations, even a mad man (Confucius 18:5).

### Self-reflection (*shu*)

The kind of self-reflection Confucius propagated involves weighing everyday events and monitoring one's behavior and attitudes (Woods and Lamond 678). People who are trying to cultivate good habits have to pay attention to what they do from day to day. They need to learn from the good examples of others as well as their own. Likewise, they need to reflect on their errors and endeavor not to repeat them. Though one could learn from others, individuals could sharpen their thinking and decision-making by becoming familiar with a wide range of scenarios and thinking about them. In this regard, it would be possible for two people to make decisions that are very different but which may nonetheless be suitable for them as individuals. Stoeckl cautions that despite this connection between self-reflection and the potential for personal transformation, "such self-reflection cannot be equated in all respects with the Western notion of individual autonomy" (28).

A person that is striving to develop moral sensitivity cannot bend to any new notion that they encounter. As Confucius notes, "the Gentleman agrees with others without being an echo. The small echoes without being in agreement" (13.23). Without power generated from self-reflection, it would be difficult for any gentleman to stand up to political or social power and to stand always for what is right. In fact, rather than seeking to follow others blindly, Wang suggests that part of the task of reflection is for the wise to explore the critical distance between themselves and others and thus appreciate how much they can learn from those that they interact with ("Confucian Selfhood" 190). As important as the individual's perspective is, Confucianists, throughout the centuries were also not unaware of the limitations of individual perspective.

The notion that individuals could immerse themselves in the Confucian classics and emerge as fully formed moral individuals came under increasing scrutiny in the sixteenth and seventeenth centuries when a group of scholar-officials began to highlight the limitations of individual perspective. To cure the deficiencies of individuals' limited perspectives, aggregations of individual scholarship were compiled and made available to students, "making these comprehensive, erudite study guides 'textual museums' available for readers to choose for themselves" (Wei, "Learning as Public Reasoning" 112).

The willingness to acknowledge that one person's "hearing, vision, mind, and knowledge" is insufficient (114), as the literati-official Xie Zhaozhe (1567-1624) had pointed out, is not to say that individuals are not important or even that their perspectives are not important. It is to say that individual perspective or opinion is limited and cannot be exchanged for personal first-hand exploration of an issue or phenomenon. So strongly did Xie Zhaozhe believe in first-hand investigation that he had no qualms about questioning one of the most respected voices in the Confucian world, Zhu Xi. As Wei reports in connection with Zhu Xi's commentaries about geysers in the area of Lu, Xie argued that it was wrong because "Zhu Xi had never come to Lu in person. However, he made a judgment based exclusively on Principles. How could he do that!" (114).

Rather than persecute those who disagreed with them, the understanding was that even highly intelligent individuals could have different viewpoints, and that, out of the collectivity of ideas, one might find a path through the thicket to some semblance of truth. This was manifest, in the seventeenth century, in the production of encyclopedias and anthologies (Wei 114) that put forth an array of ideas that were both enriching and enlivening.

## Wisdom (*zhi*)

A person who imbibes the tenets of Confucianism learns to develop discernment. Confucianism is not just about collecting maxims and principles but developing the ability to accurately judge situations and exercise proper judgment (Romar 119). Wisdom also requires that people learn from one another as they seek to become better human beings: "The Master said, When you see someone who is worthy, concentrate upon becoming their equal; when you see someone who is unworthy, use this as an opportunity to look within yourself" (Confucius 4:17). Through patient effort, one gradually develops the sensibility to make sound decisions.

Though modesty might have made Confucius reluctant to admit his excellence, he let slip that he had some good points that others could learn from. He said, "There are in a town of ten households, bound to be people who are better than I am in doing their utmost [*zhong*] and in making good on their word, but there will be no one who can compare with me in the love of learning [*haoxue*]" (5.28). The attention that Confucius occasionally drew to his love of learning was not an attempt to boast or to present himself as someone superior; rather, it was to encourage others to appreciate that whatever it was in him that they admired it had not been the product of chance, but steady, relentless effort.

The next chapter focuses on how individualism can be reflected in divergent perspectives, including some strong voices of dissent.

# *Notes*

# CHAPTER 7
# INDIVIDUALISM IN THE DIVERGENT PERSPECTIVES OF CONFUCIANISTS

Human beings can determine how they choose to stand within any society in which they are raised. According to American sociologist Anne Wortham, who discovered her sense of freedom by breaking away from some of the conventional wisdom associated with the American civil rights movement, each normal person has to be accountable for their thoughts and actions and be responsible for the heights to which they reach and the depths to which they sink. While it is difficult to challenge the notion that, "It is man's free will that individuates him" (Wortham), the social conditions surrounding a person can translate into varying degrees of struggle as one attempts to survive or thrive in that society. It is indeed possible to be free in one's mind, but we also cannot ignore the reality that society may have the power to restrain, as in slavery, or even destroy one's body if it is intolerant of dissent or challenge to the status quo. Some societies are brutal in their suppression of ideas that go against conventional wisdom, while others are more tolerant of dissent. In Confucian society, one finds throughout the centuries that, while there was a desire for harmony, there was no concomitant demand for conformity or an attempt to force everyone into one mode of thinking. As Confucius said, "Exemplary persons value harmony but not conformity; petty persons value conformity but not harmony" (Confucius 13.23).

Confucianism was open to anyone who saw value in its teachings and recognized the sacrifices that attended the pursuit of the scholarly life. Thus, we see in what has passed down through the ages as the Confucian canon, individuals who distinguished themselves in trying to preserve the moral teachings that were handed down to them. In this regard, while some became carriers of the teachings because of blood relationships to some master, this was not the sum total of what qualified one to be a carrier or promoter of the moral teachings of Confucianism.

Confucius had a son named Kong Li, also known as Boyu, whose son, Kong Ji (c. 483-402 BCE) or Master Zisi, became a prominent Confucian associated with the book, *Zhongyong*. Zisi was a student of Master Zeng (Zengzi, 505-436 BCE), a direct student of Confucius.

It is believed that Zeng was responsible for writing or compiling *The Great Learning*, which is a part of the *Classic of Rites*. And one of Zisi's disciples became the teacher of Mencius, one of the leading Confucianists of all time. "Accordingly, this lineage of teaching from Confucius, to Master Zeng, to Zisi, to his disciple and then to Mencius, is regarded now as the orthodox transmission of Confucius' teachings and known as the Si-Meng lineage" (Littlejohn 46).

What is significant about the Si-Meng lineage is that we see over many decades the preservation of some of the key tenets of Confucius's teachings, which lends a measure of continuity and perhaps a sense of authority in the eyes of those who value tradition. But the fact that there was a thread of continuity in the teachings did not mean that the individuals who carried forward the teachings lacked any sense of individuality, or that, they were perfectly in lockstep with one another. Rather, each of them was willing to examine the texts passed down from the past and to explore how they could best be applied to the realities of their day.

Mencius, for one, did not think that one had to follow blindly in the documents that had been passed down, noting that, "It would be better to have no book at all than to believe everything in it" (Eno, "Mencius" 7B3). Thus, in how Mencius, Zisi, and other individuals contributed to Confucian thought, we see evidence of individuality. Of particular interest were the divergent perspectives of some titans of Confucianism: Mencius, Gaozi, and Hsun Tsu (Xunzi).

Though they all followed in the general tenets of Confucianism, Mencius, on the one hand, and Gaozi and Hsun Tsu, on the other, all manifest individuality in the divergent trains of thought they championed especially when it came to the question of the moral nature (*xing*) of human beings. The crux of the matter was whether human beings were innately good or bad, and on this, Brindley states that Mencius provides one of the earliest and most comprehensive representations of early Chinese individualism. Mencius's mode of thought was a new way of considering the "innate moral agencies of the individual" (64). At the most basic level, Mencius saw each individual as possessing an innate tendency towards goodness and morality. He states the matter as follows:

My reason for saying that no man is devoid of a heart-mind sensitive to the suffering of others is this. Suppose a man were, suddenly, to see a young child on the verge of falling into a well. He would certainly be moved with compassionate apprehension, not because he wanted to get in the good graces of the parents, nor because he wished to win the praise of his fellow villagers or friends, nor even because he disliked the cry of the child. From this it can be seen that whoever is devoid of the heart-mind of compassion is not human, whoever is devoid of the heart-mind of shame is not human, whoever is devoid of the heart-mind of courtesy and modesty is not human, and whoever is devoid of the heart-mind of moral discretion is not human. (Eno, "Mencius" 2A6)

Mencius refuted in very strong terms an argument that had been raised by Gaozi, or Master Gao (c 420 -350 BC), that righteousness could be likened to cups and bowls fashioned out of the willow tree. Since cups and bowls could not be fashioned without doing violence to the tree, Mencius could not appreciate how an individual had to be first "violated" from an external source to pursue righteousness. To Mencius, "the motivation for moral behavior exists within each individual as a force that affirms both life and morality—a force that every individual can nourish physically on his or her own" (Brindley 66). In effect, each person, quite apart from any external influence, could determine to do the right thing.

Though Mencius believed that individuals were good at heart, he also suggested that there is an element of choice in how human beings choose to portray themselves when it comes to display or non-display of their piety. He was wary of people who made a show of virtue but did not live up to it, noting that, a person who wanted to make a show of kindness to make a name for himself could give away "a thousand chariots (for the fame of it), but if he is not really this kind of person, giving away a cup of rice or a bowl of soup will show in his face" (Eno, "Mencius" 7BII). Thus, he promoted the cultivation of virtue that was genuine and unforced. He certainly did not want "pious" people, like the man from Song, of whom it was said that he pulled at his rice shoots because he was eager for the rice to grow. After getting home, the man from Song "said to his family, 'I am worn out today; I have been helping the plants to grow'" (Littlejohn 54). His son went out of the house in a hurry, only to find that the plants had withered.

Thus, forcing moral growth was not recommended just as hastening the growth of a plant was a nonstarter. Mencius's view of Confucianism, therefore, was not one in which morality had to be beaten into people. Rather, through patient inculcation, it was hoped that the learner would imbibe the teachings and have it reflected positively in their life. As we would see a little later, this contrasted somewhat with Hsun Tsu's approach.

Another example, in Mencius's view, that highlights the insidiousness of people who make a show of piety without having the substance, is reflected in the story told about Tai Ying Chi, a local leader who said that he was not able to change over to a new tax system of ten percent and eliminate customs and market duties immediately.

Tai Ying Chi said, "What would you think if we were to make some reductions and wait till next year before putting the change fully into effect?" "Here is a man," said Mencius, "who appropriates one of his neighbor's chickens every day." Someone tells him, "This is not how an exemplary person (*junzi*) behaves." He answers, "May I reduce it to one chicken every month and wait until next year to stop altogether?" "When one realizes that something is morally wrong, one should stop it as soon as possible. Why wait for next year?" (Littlejohn 55).

If some human beings chose to make excuses for their bad behavior, it was certainly not because they did not have the agency or the conscience to do the right thing. It was a wrong path, but one that they had freely chosen.

Confucian teachings were not just for the benefit of argumentation or style. They were meant to be practical tenets for everyday interactions. In the above, Mencius makes it clear that individuals have the power to decide whether they are going to persist in wrongdoing or whether, having seen that they are on the wrong path, they would take steps to rectify the situation. Each individual has the power of agency to make moral decisions.

Mencius was also aware of the importance of the environment and its potential effect on the young. In addition to advocating for the steady development of one's character, he noted that the abundance of evil and violence could hamper the moral cultivation of young people who were exposed to them (Eno, "Mencius" 6A7, 6A9). In his own words, "The great and luxuriant trees of Ox Mountain are beautiful, but if constantly lopped by axes, can we be surprised if the mountain appears bald and ugly? The same is true of a person who repeatedly cuts down the sprouts of his moral intuitions and follows a way of immorality" (6A8). Parents, communities, and society as a whole, it can be surmised, have a responsibility to create an environment in which children can be exposed to worthy models and habits so that they can express these in their own lives.

But Mencius's hopeful view of human beings as being naturally good and predisposed to doing the right thing was not fully shared by Hsun Tsu (Xunzi), who is associated with the brand of Confucianism espoused in *The Doctrine of the Mean*. This volume appears to have been written, along with *The Great Learning*, in the Qin Dynasty, one of the most brutal periods in Chinese history. While these books acknowledge the capacity for human perfectibility, they also see the nation's leaders as the catalyst for letting virtue spread across the land (Eno, The Great Learning and the Doctrine of the Mean 7). *The Great Learning*, which is described as "a self-help manual for the aspiring ethical actor, or *junzi*" (Eno 7) states: "You already know how to be moral; all you need to learn is how to turn that knowledge into action" (Eno 7). It is primarily addressed to the individual.

In contrast to Mencius's characterization, Xunzi's view of human beings is that they are innately malleable, following whatever currents or leaders were most prominent in their time, and that, most people tended towards satisfying their base natures or characters.

Acknowledgment that the human being was beset by many competing agencies seems to have been behind Xunzi's endorsement of moral self-cultivation that relied, not on oneself, but the guidance of texts and external authorities (Brindley 90). This is not to suggest that Xunzi and Mencius were at odds at every turn. Being both followers of Confucius, they did recognize both the matter of individual choice and the matter of perfectibility through the guidance of one sort or another. But they had different approaches, which highlight the simple fact that to be Confucian was not to follow others blindly.

The book that outlines Xunzi's ideas bears his name and is divided into 32 chapters of "self-contained essays" (Littlejohn 56). Whereas Mencius believed that human beings were naturally benevolent, Xunzi believed that the natural condition of the human being is to be selfish, and that, "left to our own devices, without restrictions of external morality and law, the human inclination to selfishness will breed disorder and chaos" (57).

He believed that people had a natural tendency to do that which would profit them and that this almost certainly led to an increase in aggression and greed (Knoblock 155). To curb the envy, hate, and greed that was the natural state of the human being, Xunzi believed that an external shaping mechanism was necessary in the form of "education, morality, and law. To exercise the virtues about which Confucius taught is against our nature, and they can be realized only by great effort" (Littlejohn 57). Xunzi did not think that individuals, weak as they are, could summon the will to embark upon such change by themselves.

Xunzi also emphasized that the rites that Confucianists such as Mencius were so attached to, did not originate from heaven but were born of human ingenuity, by the sage-kings (Goldin 126). This may have been another point that Confucianists might have had difficulty countering. It followed that if the morality of the day had been invented by human beings, nothing would prevent other human beings from changing the norms of that morality. Whereas Mencius saw human beings as seeds that needed cultivation, Xunzi saw humanity as warped pieces of wood that needed steaming and pressing into a straight form. Xunzi decried the placement of faith in an impersonal heaven. Rather, he stressed that,

If there is good fortune for humans, it is because they make it happen through responsible government and a well-ordered society. Neither does Heaven make people poor or bring calamities. Heaven has no will, no mind, and thus, does not act to bring judgment or reward... *Tian* does not give up the winter because people dislike cold...*Tian* has a constant way of action. (Littlejohn 58)

Xunzi may not have had a strong belief that people always tended towards the good, but he tended towards the belief that they would be motivated to do what was necessary to improve their lives, if only out of selfish interest.

Leaders who were inclined towards magic disgusted Xunzi. He did not mind people expressing amazement at the wonders of nature, but he did not see any need for fearing nature. He would rather see leaders take responsibility to guide people towards solutions to their problems. As Xunzi notes, "When villagers fail to make provision for dikes to withstand floods, and homes and persons are lost or farmers fail to weed their crops and the harvest is slight or the government is corrupt—these are the real enemies of humankind" (58). He wanted common superstitions to be put aside in favor of using human effort to change society. It was important for Xunzi for the people around him to understand that the rites, which other Confucianists such as Mencius so highly prized, did serve a purpose, but they were human creations to serve a specific purpose; it was not helpful for the common people, in particular, to think of the rites in terms of the needs of spirits. Xunzi had an opportunity to test out his ideas, as he was involved in government service.

Confucius had already warned that leading people through reward and punishment meant that they might avoid wrongdoing, but it did not guarantee that when on their own they would allow a sense of shame and honor to guide their actions. Though Xunzi may not have approved the all-out use of rewards and punishments, his teachings, through his two disciples, eventually became so influential, and resulted in the control, mistreatment, and slaughter of people during the Qin dynasty.

Emphasizing that followers of Confucianism did not merely parrot what Confucius had said, a later strand of Confucianism, expressed in the *Book of Rites,* went further than Xunzi in pointing out that one could not depend on innate moral agency to get oneself onto the path of morality. Great emphasis was placed on externally guided self-cultivation as a complement to the potential inherent in human beings towards proper conduct. Mencius saw the moral potential within the individual, Xunzi denied such moral potential, but the *Doctrine of the Mean* accepted such potential and emphasized the need to shape it through external means such as learning from texts and acquiring instruction from moral leaders. Thus, we see that even among those that are recognized as the key figures or key schools of thought in the Confucian canon, there was individuality of thought.

Though Mencius recognized the innate positive inclination of human beings, he was also strongly averse to the kind of individualism that bordered on hedonism and the kind of communitarianism that bordered on self-abnegation. In this regard, Mencius was at pains to challenge the views of his contemporary, Yang Zhu, who Mencius believed represented egoism, and Mo Di (Mozi), who is said to have advocated "universal caring, which is tantamount to denying one's father" (Brindley 72). The middle road that Mencius takes is embodied in the saying that "Yangzi supports egoism. Even if he were to benefit the world by pulling out a single hair, he would not do it. Mozi advocates universal caring. If by exerting himself from the crown of his head to the heels of his feet he might benefit the world, he would do it ... Holding to the middle is closer to being right ... " (Confucius 17.21; 1.5). Though Mencius highlights three different positions, all of them depend on a person's own decision or sense of agency. That is, whether one chose to focus only on oneself or one chose to give oneself over to doing good deeds to all comers, to the neglect of one's own family, the choice was personal. The two extremes, in Mencius's view, were not right, but that is not to say that they are not the product of individual determination.

According to Brindley, individualism was very much a part of the debates in the period when Confucianism held sway in China. There were other philosophies and movements, some of which were far more insistent on the need for people to look inward and to "preserve or develop in an organic fashion the positive aspects of their selves, so that such individuals might prevail in the face of external threats or negative influences" (Brindley 77). For those who clung to this view, the individual needed to maintain dignity, nurture personal power and connect with cosmic authority for the benefit of the self. At the same time, some thinkers saw individualism as tending towards "selfishness and social chaos" (78) and thus, necessary to put in check.

The disagreement between Mencius and Xunzi might be summed up thus: Mencius saw human agency as being embedded in human nature whereas Xunzi saw nothing ideal about natural human tendencies and called for human effort and external authorities to enhance those weak human elements (93).

Han Feizi, also known as Han Fei, another philosopher, who had been influenced by a long list of Confucian scholars as well as non-Confucian ideas, became a strong proponent of institutional control of human beings. He believed that, left to their own devices, human beings were apt to engage in negative behaviors that were harmful to the society. His basic belief, captured in an eponymous book, *Han Feizi*, was that "since humans are fundamentally not malleable, and since most are neither wise nor moral, strict and punitive measures are needed to maintain social order" (95). He believed that people who were born with some crooked tendencies in them would tend to become crooked while those that had been born with some straight tendencies had a good chance of being straight.

In effect, "Although individual natures are indeed differentiated, they are each fixed and not responsive to processes of education and cultivation that try to change them. In other words, one's endowment very much defines one's self" (95). Han Feizi's view, which denies the possibility of human perfectibility through personal determination is not considered to be a mainstream Confucian viewpoint. So far does he drift from Confucian orthodoxy, which discourages the use of punishment in regulating society, that he is associated with the Legalist school, reflected in one of his statements, that: "People inherently [grow] proud with affection (*ai*), yet they obey might" (99). The Legalist school believed that the Confucian school, by giving individuals the freedom to choose virtue and to promote such virtues through persuasion, rather than force, was harming society since most people could not be trusted to choose the path of goodness. Rather, by having a prescribed set of rules that all people had to adhere to, even though their autonomy and agency might come under pressure, it was a surer path to having peace and order in the society. Though some see the Confucian promotion of rituals and study as taking away from an individual's freedom, the Legalists were worse in this regard, having had no qualms about using punishment to get people to do what they believed to be good for society.

Throughout Chinese history, there were individuals, who through the force of their intellect or persuasive powers, managed to stake a place for themselves as contributors to the spread or entrenchment of Confucianism. One such person was Han Yu (768- 824 AD). To rejuvenate Confucianism, which had become marginalized and less influential, Han Yu wrote *The Original Way* as a means to redirect the attention of the society back to Confucianism. He must have succeeded, for it has been noted that "Since Mencius there has been nothing of value except the single essay *The Original Way*" (Graham 162). But Han Yu was himself criticized as he continually linked Confucianism to the Chinese character, thus inviting charges of ethnocentrism. He saw aspects of Buddhism as nothing but superstition and was distressed when the emperor in his day participated in a Buddhist procession that included what he saw as practices based purely on superstition. Han Yu's strident criticism of the emperor did not go unnoticed. "The emperor's response was swift and decisive. Han Yu was banished to the farthest southern reaches of China, sent to Chaozhou in 819 as an exile" (Littlejohn 111). In a few decades, however, the campaign for the destruction of Buddhism and Daoism that Han Yu had called for, materialized.

The power vacuum following the fall of the T'ang dynasty led to the proliferation of warlords, each trying to assert himself in one corner of the land or another. In the Song dynasty (960-1279 AD), which followed the T'ang, the calls that Han Yu had made for spreading knowledge of Confucianism began to be heeded. The Song period has been described as the renaissance period of Confucianism (115). From the eleventh century to the late seventeenth century, among Chinese people, Confucianism became the dominant worldview, with the Ming Dynasty (1368-1644) alone lasting over three hundred years and covering the whole of China. One person who raised this issue in his time was Cheng Hao (1032-1085), who believed that indeed, anyone who put their mind to it, could become a sage. As he noted,

...Their education should proceed from the lesser learning of scattering water, sweeping, receiving and responding to fulfilling their filial piety, fraternity, loyalty, and honesty, being well-rounded in rites (*li*) and music; this is the way by which they should be enticed, pulled in, gradually polished, and completed. All this has sequenced order. The main point is choosing good and improving the self, to arrive at transforming the whole world. This is the way by which villagers can become sages. When their learning and conduct both [accord] perfectly with these their virtue may be considered complete. (Richey 122-123)

At various points, some individuals emerged as either the greatest champions of Confucianism or its greatest critics. Some of these individual voices resonated far and wide, either because the person took the initiative to write down their ideas or because others were able to capture the ideas in writing. From the foregoing, it is clear that Confucianists shared knowledge of the importance of leading a moral life, but their understanding of the natural endowments of the human being left room for disputation.

To sum up this chapter, Mencius believed that the individual was naturally good and would almost without coercion tend toward the good; he also rejected selfishness and greed. Other philosophers who had had the benefit of some of the same Confucian ethos of self-cultivation, including Gaozi, Hsun Tsu, and Han Fei, all saw individuals as almost being crooked from the start, and thus, in need of a strong hand to straighten them up, whether in the form of texts and training (Hsun Tsu) or the mighty hand of the law (Han Fei).

The purpose of this chapter was to highlight a few individuals who loom large within the pantheons of Confucianism. Through discussion and public presentation of ideas, all these titans were able to have their say. The next chapter focuses primarily on how individualism in Confucianism is further manifested in the matter of individual responsibility.

# Notes

# CHAPTER 8
# THE MATTER OF INDIVIDUAL RESPONSIBILITY

In the article, "On Economic Individualism," philosopher Tibor R. Machan argues that it is in the nature of human beings to choose how they conduct themselves, aware that these actions can either lead them towards moral excellence or ruin (149). He makes this comment about all human beings and further asserts that, in consequence, "each man must be considered individually, for only he can be held responsible or given credit for making his choices" (150). Considering that individuals live within communities and societies that have rules, it would also be unfair to usher individuals into a community and leave them without any guidance as to how to conduct themselves, especially when community norms might mean that those who violate such norms could be subject to the wrath and censure of the community.

When it comes to Confucian society, as indeed it is

with other societies, individuals are taught from an early age about how they can best survive within the community. Individuals are not taught to reject out of hand the connections of kinship that they have inherited.

Kim Sungmoon, whose research interests run the gamut from democratic and constitutional theory to Confucianism and East Asian political thought, argues that the "Confucian self is a social self, not a self-choosing autonomous individual" (Kim Confucian Democracy 29). Kim goes on to explain that the relationship between self and society is not only harmonious but also mutually constitutive (37). From this psychosocial argument placed in a historical context, we learn that the individual is not perpetually, intentionally, or eagerly attempting to separate himself from society to feel fulfilled.

Rather, by the process of natural development and growth in the society, the individual is shaped with near-constant awareness of the need to pay heed to both self and others. In this regard, Charlene Tan believes that, rather than just catering to the needs of the society, Confucius's teachings are geared towards pulling together the strands of moral, aesthetic, and spiritual elements of the individual. For it would seem to be unfair, for example, to punish a child, an individual, for transgressing a rule to which the child has not previously been apprised. This also probably explains the clash that existed between Confucianists, who believed in the patient cultivation of the sensibilities of the individual, and Legalists, who saw strict punishment as the way to regulate society.

*The Doctrine of the Mean* echoes one of the most important ideas of Confucianism, namely, looking to oneself rather than blaming others: "In failing to hit the bull's eye, look for the reason inside of yourself and not elsewhere" (Littlejohn 4). Confucianism did not offer a place for unnecessary excuses but rather taught that each person was in part "responsible for dealing with the environmental factors that prevented his Heavenly gifts from functioning, and for turning his capabilities into actual practice" (Munro The Concept of Man 90). In a world where it was common knowledge that education was a means to self-mastery, self-respect, and societal respect, some people would freely choose to pick up a book while others would neglect to do the same.

Even the destitute were not unaware of what it could mean for them if they chose the book over the plow, and there are many instances in Chinese history, where the lowliest of the low rose to the highest echelons of society. For those with lofty aspirations, the decision had to be made at some point in their early lives, to sacrifice personal comfort, to brave loneliness and solitude, and focus on memorization and study, and to continually commune with other members of the society that had similarly chosen the path of study and moral perfectibility.

Confucianism, therefore, sought to cultivate adult human beings, that is, individuals who took responsibility for their actions, and more importantly, thought ahead before taking any action. And having taken action, to take responsibility for the consequences. This meant that the individual could not take refuge in the circumstances of their birth or blame peer pressure. Thus, to some extent, Confucianism accorded with Anne Wortham's (1975) conception that, while an individual "has no choice about his need for oxygen…he can choose to pollute his mind with the smog of doubts, fears, and rationalities; or he can keep his mind filtered with continuous inquiry, knowledge, and validation." But human beings do not live as islands apart; they live in environments that can have an impact upon them. How they choose to respond, however, depends to some extent on the individual.

Confucianism did not place all the responsibility for a person's development on the individual. As Munro notes, "Teachers acted as guides and models, but each man had to exert his own effort, consistently emulating the attitude and behavior of the model" (The Concept of Man 91). Confucianism recognized the necessity of useful guides, just as parents would guide a child that was learning to walk. Ultimately, the child had to do the walking.

That the individual can be affected by their environment and that the individual has the power to choose how they deal with it is embodied in the story of Mencius's mother. How she sought a more conducive environment for the nurturance of her son is evidence of the power of individual decision-making as an element of Confucianism. Mencius's father died when the child was very young. The poor mother found lodging near a cemetery. As a boy, Mencius played among the graves and sometimes pretended to perform burials. The mother decided that this was not a fitting environment to raise her boy. Their next place of abode was near a marketplace, where the boy, observing the interactions between merchants and their customers, played at being a tradesman.

In an era when merchants were not judged to be the most upright of human beings, the mother again uprooted herself and her son, and moved near a schoolhouse. In this new environment, the child played at being a student and became a diligent one. This mother, even in her lowly, dejected state, was free to make autonomous decisions that favored herself and her son. This is recounted as part of the Confucian canon of stories meant to inspire families and children towards wise decision-making and respect for education. Inadvertently, it illustrates the power of individuality and the power to decide the direction of one's life. It illustrates that in Confucian society, each individual had the agency to cultivate the conditions within which they could nurture their potential as human beings.

In addition to the benefit that individuals could attain by learning from others, Confucianism also enjoined people to look within themselves. This is reflected in the Confucian saying that when one encountered a bad person, one ought to turn one's gaze inward. This self-analysis between what is outside and what is within was also a precursor to developing the habit of mind of living in tranquility even when the world around remained turbulent. As Munro writes, "Mental tranquility was one of the attributes of the good life, and self-examination was a step that preceded it" (The Concept of Man 95). This was not the kind of self-examination that could be outsourced to a teacher, parent, or friend.

Individuals had to face themselves, and some of the reflections made in isolation or the serenity of the individual mind might later on become reflections of the person's character in the social world. Thus, taking the time to get to know one's mind, to take stock of one's behavior, and to make decisions on what to strengthen and what to excise, point to the sense of independence that individuals steeped in the teachings of Confucianism carried with them in the course of learning or interacting with family and friends.

# *Notes*

# CHAPTER 9
# THE INDIVIDUAL'S RELATIONSHIP TO THE FAMILY

There is no question that the family, as the bedrock of society, is given a great deal of attention and consideration in Confucianism. But, even within the family, the matter of individuality is not lost. As indicated earlier, in Confucianism, each individual has a special relationship with other individuals in the family based on what role they occupy, be it father, mother, son, daughter, elder brother, younger sister, and the like. Even though the family is extolled, Confucianism does not shrink from pointing out some of the potential shortcomings of a family unit.

In this regard, on the issue of aligning one's household as mentioned in *The Great Learning*, the point is made that all human beings are biased towards one thing or another, whether these be our children or those we dislike. Parents, for example, are quite often unwilling to acknowledge their children's faults. Aligning one's household suggests being aware of this bias and perhaps considering it in one's dealings. Tu Weiming expresses it much more clearly when he notes that for the self to grow and achieve its full potential "it needs to learn to transcend egoism, nepotism, parochialism, communalism, and anthropocentrism" ("Confucian Humanism in Perspective" 336). A society in which people only care about themselves or what is their own, is one that cannot long remain cohesive; rather, fostering a society in which people care about one another and are willing to extend the notion of fairness to their fellow compatriots promises to be a society in which anyone, native-born or visitor, might perhaps feel at ease.

One element of individualism is the opportunity for privacy. The opportunity to be with one's family and, for a period, remain apart from the rest of the society, can be linked to the matter of individuality if the family is seen, in one sense, as a unit. In ancient China, the family, which played the most elemental role in an individual's development, did not stand in opposition to the state, but rather, maintained a reciprocal relationship to it (Doh 148). In truth, the interest of the state superseded that of individuals or the family (Bell Confucian Political Ethics 204). Even so, under Confucianism, the spirit of a family's cooperation extended to civic organizations, which also cooperated rather than competed with the state.

People who live together and share kinship bonds,

both by physical proximity and by blood, recognize that the well-being of one "depends on the efforts of the whole family or group. If each person follows group norms and acts in its interests, the group will be harmonious and prosperous" (Leung 231). In this regard, the success of the group and the success of the individual are intertwined.

While most people would agree that family members should be supportive of one another, Confucius is sometimes seen as going too far. One of the most shocking conversations in the *Analects* relates to what one should do if one's father has stolen a sheep. Confucius argued that fathers and sons should shield one another (Confucius 13:18). Though some might argue that Confucius is wrong on this score and that it is indefensible, Klaus Mühlhahn points out that this was a case in which an individual could be seen to be enfolded into the family unit. Thus, for matters of law enforcement, it was unacceptable for the ruler to pit family members against one another in the name of justice.

Knowing that the conduct of one reflects on all in the public sphere, a family is likely to "supervise the behavior of its own members and act on infractions" (Mühlhahn 19) rather than delegate this delicate moral matter to the outside world. Individual members of the family could never stop watching out for other members of the family because, each of them, in a moment of lassitude, might do something that might bring disrepute upon the family as a whole.

Confucius lived in a time when such an accusation, such as stealing another's property, could lead to very harsh repercussions. Confucius might have wanted the son in question to remonstrate with the father in private (Rainey 26). In fact, Confucius gives many examples of the need for a son to remonstrate with the father or for an advisor to remonstrate with the leader. Confucianism recognized that a minister or son was to some extent likely to follow orders from a king or the person's father without directly questioning the authority figure. This appears to be a clear case of erasing another person's individuality. Even so, Xunzi recognizes that "such a duty may be overridden if it is needed to correct some especially grave error in these orders" (Wong 36). For example, in the *Hsiao Ching*, referring to the potential for leaders to stray, and the need for them to have wise counsel, we read:

If the prince of a state had five such ministers, though his measures be equally wrong, he would not lose his state; if a great officer had three, he would not, in a similar case, lose (the headship of) his clan; if an inferior officer had a friend who would remonstrate with him, a good name would not cease to be connected with his character. (Legge The Sacred Books of China 484)

Presumably, such leaders would survive any difficulties as long as there were wise individuals to help set them on the right path. The *Hsiao Ching* (*The Classic of Filial Piety*) also notes that as important as such criticism might be, the critic needs to do so with sensitivity and tact, and not to press the matter to the point of jeopardizing the relationship with the object of the criticism. This does not mean condoning bad behavior; it just shows the need, in delicate matters particularly, to protect the feelings of people who may already have been wounded by self-recrimination.

On the one hand, we see in the Confucian advice for the need of counsel the recognition that the experiences of individuals, when properly shared, can help make the society a better place. Each individual has unique experiences going through life that might not necessarily be open to others but could nevertheless become instructive. So, the more opportunities one has to surround oneself with wise and thoughtful people, the better. On the other hand, the call for sensitivity recognizes the fragile nature of the human ego and the need to ensure that too much pressure is not put on any individual to the point of doing damage to that person's psyche.

When Zengzi questioned Confucius about the great emperors of the past, Confucius responded that those revered emperors were successful because they knew "how to live with reverence for their families (*xiao*)" (Littlejohn 43). The idea was that rulers who had a love for their parents would know the value of other people's parents to them. Likewise, government officials who had respect for their parents, it was presumed, would have fellow feeling for other people's parents and thus treat everyone with respect. As Ames and Rosemont explain,

Those who are truly able to serve their parents are not arrogant in high station, are not rebellious in a subordinate position, and are not contentious when only one among many...Until these three attitudes—arrogance, defiance, and contentiousness—are set aside, even though someone were to feed their parents on beef, mutton, and pork, they still could not be deemed filial. (111)

Even though one of the highest ideals of Confucianism was to maintain harmony, this was not meant to be achieved by magic. Rather, each individual was to play their part, by seeing others as individuals worthy of respect, starting of course, from the home. Though equality of worth and differences in effort have been touched upon, the next chapter focuses on how differences become more pronounced among individuals, leading to hierarchy. This, however, supports rather than negates the notion that people have a sense of individuality.

# Notes

# CHAPTER 10
# CONFUCIAN HIERARCHY, LEADERSHIP, AND INDIVIDUALISM

The Confucian emphasis on hierarchy has sometimes come under criticism and is especially considered outdated in the modern world (Yuen 99), the late 20th century and early 21st century. Confucian support for hierarchy recognizes that while individuals might be equal, both the environment and differences in individual effort can conspire to elevate some individuals above others.

Confucianists were opposed to "hereditary privilege" (Munro The Concept of Man 3), but believed that all men had an evaluative mind, which some used to a greater extent than others, and thus, creating "an aristocracy of merit" (14). And the age of turmoil in which Confucius lived required the most competent people, regardless of background, who could help steer the ship of state to success. Those who saw the opportunity to discipline themselves and take advantage of the resources around them, including the acquisition of knowledge, were able to journey towards the possible dream of assuming roles as political counselors, and with that, garner the associated honor and glory.

Confucius's statement, that lords should be lords and fathers should be fathers, is one of the examples of distinctions drawn among men (Confucius 12.11). Whereas the father was the leader in the home because of his age and greater experience, so the lords had the responsibility of ensuring that those in their realm, had the necessities of life and the protection they deserved. Each person, regardless of position, had to understand how they could contribute to making society a successful one. It was taken for granted in Confucian society that, for the sake of harmony, individuals had to observe social obligations and that, the effort towards mastery of the ritual proprieties of the culture could help maintain the five cardinal relationships: "ruler-subject, parent-child, husband-wife, elder-younger, and friend-friend" (Munro Individualism & Holism 104). Education and the acquisition of cultural knowledge were deemed necessary for a person to properly manage and navigate these relationships.

While Confucianism had a lot of advice for individuals who sought to climb the "social ladder," it also had plenty of advice for rulers, noting, for example, that if a leader's conduct is correct, then, the government will work well while if the leader's conduct is wanting, "he may give orders but will not be obeyed" (Confucius 13:6). Also, the injunction for the young to obey the old and for women to obey men is seen by some as a negative feature of Confucianism. But Confucius nowhere asked for the old to oppress the young or for men to oppress women. He asks for the old to show kindness to the young.

Also, when Mencius says that "those who labor with their minds govern others, while those who labor with their strength are governed by others" (Mencius 3A:4), this is not a prescription for how the world ought to be. It is a simple observation by an astute teacher who realizes that when it comes to the organization of a community or the management of a society, brawn alone is not enough for one to be a leader. It is for this very reason that kings and emperors sought advisors, who were not chosen for their physical strength but their intelligence, insight, and discernment. This same Mencius did not automatically put leaders first. He believed that the people came first, then country, after which came the sovereign (6B:14). In this respect, the value of the individual did not depend on the position that the person occupied on the societal hierarchy.

*The Great Learning* placed a great deal of responsibility upon leaders, who were to be seen as trustees of the well-being of the people. In this respect, the ruler was supposed to cultivate the highest virtue and pave the way for the subjects to do the same. The advice that the ruler must take care of the subjects as though they were watching over an infant, illustrates the loving attention that was expected of the leader towards their subjects. Zengzi said, "When a ruler loves what the people love, and hates what the people hate, then is he what is called the parent of the people" (Li, The Sage and the Second Sex 119). It is expected that good parents would only do what is good for their children. Thus, the idea of the leader as the parent is an apt one, connoting care, concern, and cultivation of the best that is in the child or the subject, and emphasizing that every individual entrusted to the care of the leader was precious and needed to be valued as such.

In a society that suppresses the individuality of its members, the kind of individual agency that often results in some members distinguishing themselves far above others might be absent or severely blunted. But this was not the case with Confucianism. The elements for self-cultivation were practically available to all within the society, though in fairness, people of more comfortable means would have been in a much better position to avail themselves of these opportunities. In any case, in the past as in our day, every ruler worries about how they can keep their position, and perhaps expand their kingdom. In addition to building a fighting apparatus that can keep enemies or potential enemies at bay, leaders usually want to have the benefit of wise counsel around them so that they do not take precipitous decisions. In that sense, people with insight, and a sense of strategy, have always been in high demand around courts. The whole point of leadership under Confucianism was that the leader had to lead by example. The leader's conduct was to be the best advertisement for the rightness of their approach (Confucius 13.1). In addition to modeling good behavior for others to follow (Munro The Concept of Man xii), the Confucian leader inspires rather than pressures others into submission. In effect, "A Confucian leader does not force people to do and say right things, but cultivates people to think and do things in the right way" (Helin et al. 55). This includes dealing with people so that they feel included, not isolated. In this respect, the dialogues between Confucius and his disciples, as reflected in the *Analects*, show a kind and considerate teacher, not someone that people feared to be around.

Confucius lived in a world in which there was always the threat of war. He was not a pacifist, but he did not see the antidote to war as creating bigger and better weapons. Rather, he sought to get at the root of evil and bad behavior, and perhaps, then, remove the need for war in the first place. In everyday life, Confucianists believed that having a good government that catered to the welfare of all was wholly dependent upon "securing the right person, the exemplary person as ruler" (Littlejohn 41). As the *Classic of Poetry* notes, "Harboring the highest virtue (*de*) in one's breast there is no need for loud words or intimidating looks…The influence of virtue is as light as a feather" (41). Through self-correction and self-monitoring, a serious Confucianist that continually pursues the path of righteousness is unlikely to descend into the kind of hubris that is often the downfall of many a great person.

As noted earlier, the respect that Confucius commands not only in China but sometimes, as the only major Chinese figure that many people outside of China, can name, might make it seem as though he was a beloved figure both in his life and after. The ethical conduct that Confucius espoused, which might sound to modern ears, so lucid and reasonable, did not necessarily fall kindly upon the ears of the many leaders of factions in his time. And yet, he strove to do nothing more than "to make the human being good—a good father, a good mother, a good son, a good daughter, a good friend, a good citizen" (Dawson vi). The principles were to serve the individual well whether in their interactions with another human being or in their dealings with a larger group of people.

The models of excellence and virtue that Confucius looked up to were figures that had been renowned not just for their knowledge, but for their promotion of peace, harmony, and prosperity. As Ni notes, the highest aim of a Confucianist is "to become a sage rather than just to be a normal person" (340). Lofty as that goal might be, Confucius was not unaware that every human being could make progress on that road to perfect virtue that few ever attain. He, having been born without a silver spoon in his mouth, had nevertheless, by patient striving, been able to acquire the habits of mind and learning that had made him a teacher with dozens of followers. His life, then, could serve as an example that, with some effort, anyone could make their own.

Schools and communities of learners such as that of Confucius were meant to express aspects of public opinion because it was from this pool of scholars and intellectuals that the government drew its supply of officials. In another sense, these schools could become centers of admonition as well as support to the government. As Shils writes, "The belief that the highly educated should take on responsibilities entailing critical and positive participation in the exercise of governmental authority is central to Confucianism" (8). This meant that those who had the opportunity to sharpen their moral and intellectual sensibilities did not have to hold back from taking leadership positions in the same way that those whose backgrounds fitted them for other occupations in the society such as farming and the artisanal trades might have gravitated towards those options.

Some researchers, such as the Japanese sinologist Hattori Unokichi, have stated that Confucianism is not a practical philosophy (Cheng, New Dimensions 424), possibly because pursuers of philosophical truths such as Confucius were fixated on bringing some elusive form of peace to the land. Confucius's view of humaneness, however, was not just a speculative endeavor. Rather, it was rooted in concrete practice. For example, when one of his disciples, Zixia, asked him a question about this very idea of speculation on heavenly things, Confucius told him: "Learn broadly yet be focused on your purposes; inquire with urgency yet reflect closely on the question at hand—humaneness (*ren*) lies simply in this" (Confucius 19.6).

Confucius's admonition that his followers take no responsibility for planning policies of an office that they do not hold (8.14, 14.26) makes it appear as though Confucius and his followers were not supposed to take any interest at all in government. This statement and others, however, appear to be statements of caution. After all, if one is not in office and one makes proposals that one is not in a position to carry out, of what benefit is it?

Knowing especially the danger that could befall critics of powerful leaders, Confucius offers the following advice: "When the Way prevails in the world, governing does not lie in the hands of the ministers; when the Way prevails in the world, the common people do not debate affairs of the state" (Confucius 16.2; Ames and Rosemont 197). This is not to suggest that the ministers do nothing at all. Rather, it suggests that when everything is aligned for the better, and the ministers are planning and doing what needs doing, they do not live in a state of crisis. As well, the common people, who have so much to worry about in their daily lives do not have to be concerned about the state of the land. Of course, in times of crisis, everyone, including the common people, might be drawn towards political concerns.

Confucius warned *junzi* about serving a corrupt government. He advised his followers not to enter a state that was in crisis and not to waste time in one that was engulfed in revolt. He counseled them to be visible when the way of goodness was being universally practiced in the world and to remain hidden when this was not the case. "It is a disgrace to remain poor and without rank when the way prevails in the state; it is a disgrace to be wealthy and of noble rank when it does not" (Confucius 8.13). This suggests that in a land where the Way prevails, the leaders would know enough to ensure that the wise are taken care of, in fact, that all are taken care of. No one, therefore, ought to be poor in a land where goodness prevails.

On the other hand, in a corrupt land, being wealthy might suggest that one is either corrupt or that one is turning a blind eye to the sufferings of others. A good government is one that cares not only about the wealthy but also about the common people. In effect, if the common people were to lose their confidence in the government or their leaders, the community could not long endure (12.7). Ideally, the government would strive for harmony with the people, so that the two are not on different paths. As Confucius warns, "People who have chosen different ways (*Dao*) cannot make plans together" (15.40). So, individuals have to pay attention to those with whom they frequently commune.

In any case, those who adhered to Confucianism had to be prepared to estrange themselves from a political authority that was immoral in its outlook. In this regard, Confucius suggested that a person like Yan Hui, one of his followers who was quite passionate about his studies, could be happy enough living on his small piece of land and enjoy the peace of mind of an independent person rather than tether himself to some corrupt leader because of the desire to live a luxurious lifestyle.

In Chapter 25 and 27 of *The Zhuangzi*, the spirit of individualism and autonomy evident in the lives of Qu Boyu and Confucius are presented. Of Confucius, it is said that "growing up to his sixty years old, he has changed sixty times. There was nothing that he called right at the beginning that had not been rejected as wrong by himself in the end" (Keqian 456). Both Boyu and Confucius are presented as dynamic beings with the agency to change rather than being fixed in character or subject to the dictates of others. The individualism that Zhuangzi, known for Daoist philosophy, espoused was spiritual and did not, therefore, clash strongly with Confucianism. But the point is that even Zhuangzi recognized that Confucius and thus, Confucianism, were not without aspects of individualism.

In the *Analects*, three types of people are identified. One is the apprentice (*shi*), the person who has come to learn from the more experienced and more knowledgeable; the second is the exemplary person (*junzi*), and the third is the sage (*sheng ren*). The goal of a disciple, not surprisingly, is to grow steadily to become a *junzi*, a person who is described in reverential terms:

> While he is still capable of anger in the presence of inappropriateness and concomitant injustice, he is in his person tranquil. He knows many rituals and much music, and performs all of his functions not only with skill but also with grace, dignity, and beauty...He is still filial towards his parents, and elders but now takes all under Heaven and his dwelling. (Littlejohn 32)

The exemplary person might be a role model of sorts, because his way of life, in service to his community, makes him worthy of emulation.

Exemplary men, who are leaders for the wisdom that they impart, strive daily to do what is right or appropriate and to pay attention to themselves; they are not driven by desire for glitter or shiny objects. Rather, they seek to make their deeds match their words (Confucius 14.27). They do not seek flattery from others and are distressed if they fall short of the ideals that they so greatly cherish. In theory, the *junzi*, as an individual, does not follow this strict path of learning and practice because of the potential for wealth. As the *Analects* say, "Wealth and rank are what people want, but if they are the consequence of deviating from the Way (*Dao*), I would have no part in them. Poverty and disgrace are what people deplore, but if they are the consequence of staying on the Way, I would not avoid them" (Confucius 4.5). Exemplary people follow a path of continual self-examination and make demands of themselves rather than blaming others for their deficiencies.

It was particularly desirable for those at the top of society to cultivate themselves into exemplary persons. This is because a ruler with the virtues that Confucianism espouses could influence the society to aspire towards moral excellence. The sage is an even rarer species of human being. Sages have also gone through the steps of becoming exemplary people but they are above and beyond, almost imbued with some spiritual quality. Confucius said, "I will never get to meet a sage. I would be content to meet an exemplary person" (Confucius 7.26). And when people tried to pin the term "sage" on him, Confucius sought to wiggle out of it, saying, "How would I dare to consider myself a sage or *ren*? What can be said about me is that I continue my studies without respite and instruct others without growing weary—is this not me?" (Confucius 7.34). Perhaps, it was his way of saying that we should not be greedy for titles but focus on the job that most needs to be done.

The idea of propriety and hierarchy that Confucianism valued, as it turns out, was antithetical to the perspective of the Daoist philosopher, Chuang Tzu, who delighted in poking fun at both the Confucianists and the Legalists. From the viewpoint of Chuang Tzu, the Confucian ideal of "socialization through the external process of ritual and the learning of the classics constituted the imposition of something extrinsic on top of the inner self" (Munro Individualism and Holism 104). Thus, though one determined to become a Confucian scholar might, of his own accord, become immersed in the classics, Chuang Tzu viewed this as possibly limiting the individual's human potential. In fact, "Chuang Tzu's arguments imply that in order to find the free and autonomous self, one has to break free from the institutions and conventions of the social world" (105). In comparison to the Confucianists, the Daoists were fierce about protecting their individualism and were not averse to staying apart from society, living as hermits.

Even the Confucian view of a sage or the scholar as a dignified or wise person was seen by Chuang Tzu as taking something from human individuality, raising the question of why someone who was "ugly, repulsive, and irreverent" (105) could not simultaneously be wise or the possessor of something of value. Thus, though there were elements of Confucianism that valued individual decision-making and human agency, from the viewpoint of Chuang Tzu, Confucians were not as free as they might have imagined themselves to be. After all, as Chuang Tzu surmised, the truly ambitious Confucian, all through life, could be dedicated to a prescribed way of life that might not necessarily accord with their true heart.

Be that as it may, Confucius's guidance to his followers and leaders included adhering to the correct use of language, nonsupport for hereditary privileges, promotion of effort, and pursuit of a moral core as the birthright of any human being. Confucius's endless quest for the principles that would lead to good government, and thus, greater happiness for all, combine an understanding of the value of each individual with the need for social harmony.

## Notes

# CHAPTER 11
# WOMEN, CONFUCIANISM, AND INDIVIDUALITY

For those who think of Confucianism in purely communitarian terms, women may be virtually invisible. But then, even for those who are willing to accept that there was a measure of individuality in Confucianism, the names that loom largest in the Confucian world are those of men such as Confucius and Mencius. Even among Chinese, during the period of the May Fourth Movement in the early part of the twentieth century, a new crop of intellectuals lamented the weak position of China vis-à-vis some Western nations; some blamed Confucianism for many societal ills, including the inferiority of women, particularly rural women (Rosenlee 1). Surface appearances may lend credence to such suspicions, but a deeper study reveals that the matter is much more complex, and that, throughout Confucian society, despite the gender role division, women were able to make their marks in various spheres, including transcending the traditional domestic sphere.

Critics of Confucianism often latch on to the admonition that a woman should obey her father when young, obey her husband while married, and obey her son when in old age, to argue that Confucianism had no respect for women. In this, they may be judging the past by the yardstick of today. In Confucianism, attention was paid to the education of women, and the obedience that was requested of women was not synonymous with a right for the males to abuse the women in their lives. While men, whether as political leaders or arbiters of morality, often garnered greater attention, some individuals, like Mencius, spoke about or wrote about the influence that their mothers had had on them (De Bary and Bloom, Sources of Chinese Tradition 820). Some women, in their own right, became famous for the texts they wrote on how other women might best handle their wifely duties. In other words, the individuality of women was not obscured by their supposed position of inferiority.

One of the most popular books that served this purpose, called *Biographies of Exemplary Women*, edited by Liu Xiang (79 BCE), was in almost continual use for 2,000 years. Among the categories of women that were featured were, 1) Matronly Models, 2) Worthy and Enlightened, 3) Benevolent and Wise, 4) Chaste and Obedient, 5) Principled and Righteous, 6) Accomplished Speakers, and 7) Depraved Favorites. We see in these manuals the elevation of particular types of women, not as groups, but as individuals who exemplified certain noble characteristics.

To be sure, some of the materials that were written for women were written by men. These were often more directly didactic in approach, which is to say, preachy. On the other hand, when women wrote for themselves, it conveyed "spiritual and emotional power, steadfast resolve, hardhearted practical reasoning, and dazzling creativity" (Mann and Cheng 7). In principle, the domestic was supposed to be the domain of women, but there are indications that some women were able to transcend this limitation, especially when it comes to two prominent areas in which they excelled: fiction writing and random jottings (4). In both of these, though the agents of such works might have come from the higher classes, it shows, in any case, that women were able to carve out time and space to cultivate their talents and to unleash the creative products of their imaginations on the society.

Just as men needed to be channeled into uprightness through self-cultivation, women were encouraged to uphold morality. Liu Xiang's *Traditions of Exemplary Women* suggests that Confucianism recognized the perfectibility of both men and women and the value of effort and continual self-reflection. Although the harsh life of Chinese women throughout history, including foot-binding and widow suicides, have often been connected to Confucianism, in reality,

Oppression of women is not embedded in the central teachings of Confucius and in the Zisi-Mencius lineage or in Xunzi. Moreover, the fundamental teachings of the pre-Han founders of Confucianism actually support a human, not gender-based spiritual way.

There is gender equality in the pursuit of the Confucian Way. (Littlejohn 75)

Ban Gu, a court historian in the Han Dynasty, who composed the *Comprehensive Discussions in the White Tiger Hall*, had a younger sister named Ban Zhao (c 45-116 CE) who was a leading Confucianist in her own right. When her brother died, she took his place by serving as Imperial Historian under Emperor Han Hedi (r. 88-105 C.E.). The work that she completed, known as *History of the Farmer Han*, is "generally regarded as second in historical significance only to that of Sima Qian" (75). We see in both the examples of Liu Xiang and Ban Zhao that women who so desired, particularly those at the upper echelons of the society, were able to cultivate their talents, literary and otherwise, and thus nurture their individuality. There was no proscription in Confucianism on these women either developing their literary skills or in their propagating to others the knowledge and experience that they had acquired.

Ban Zhao was educated by her mother initially. She

married young, at the age of fourteen. Following the death of her husband at an early age, she did not remarry. Rather, she poured her energy into her scholarship. In addition to composing a commentary on the *Biographies of Exemplary Women*, she also wrote her most famous book, *Precepts for Women*, which shared the proper feminine virtue and behavior in the Confucian Way. In this book, Ban Zhao encouraged not only humility and industriousness but also uprightness and an exemplary moral character. But her advice was not only for women. She provided timely advice for men that touched on how they could be good husbands.

The basic idea, which fits in with the notion of harmony, was for men to learn to "control" women and for women to serve men. But they had to respect each other. As Ban Zhao wrote, "Now for self-culture nothing equals respect for others. To counteract firmness nothing equals compliance. Consequently, it can be said that the Way of respect and acquiescence is man's most important principle of conduct" (78). The four qualifications for women were as follows:

a) womanly virtue,
b) womanly words,
c) womanly bearing, and
d) womanly work.

Also, modesty, the use of respectful language, cleanliness, and obedience to their mother-in-law were recommended. She advised, "Let a woman not act contrary to the wishes and opinions of her parents-in-law about right and wrong; let her not dispute with them over what is straight and what is crooked. Such docility may be called obedience which sacrifices personal opinion" (79). It is clear from this advice that Ban Zhao did not give unfettered license to the wife to assert herself and to contradict the senior members of the family into which she was now embedded. Advising a woman to suppress her viewpoint is certainly indefensible in this modern age and reveals that there were limits to the kind of individualism that Confucianism advocated. But then, a wife who made a habit of contradicting her parents-in-law, while possibly right, might set herself up for unnecessary pain and years of heartache and conflict. Thus, Ban Zhao's advice, restrictive and unfair as it might seem, ends up trading a measure of individuality for harmony.

Though Ban Zhao was not from an imperial clan, her talents as a writer caught the attention of the Court, where she was invited to reside until her death at an advanced age. Evidence of the esteem that was accorded her can be seen in the fact that when she died, not only did the Empress Dowager herself go into mourning but also she ordered functionaries of the court to make the necessary funeral arrangements and to represent her at the rites. As Brown writes, "This unusually high-profile funeral for a female scholar is the most eloquent possible testimony to Ban Zhao's reputation and influence at the time of her death" (229). It is further testimony that there was room in Confucianism for talented people of either gender to be given their due and to be held up as exemplars.

Within Confucianism, indeed, men have often been at the forefront. This was the case also when it came to inheritance, as ideas on succession linked the inheritance of property to ritual practices that the male heir would perform as sacrifices to the departed parent. While some Confucian reformers sometimes challenged women's rights to property, in general, they acknowledged the importance and centrality of women, particularly widows, in maintaining the estates of their departed husbands.

In the Sung era, senior wives who had successfully managed their households were eulogized at their death (Birge 29). Besides, the admonition by some Confucian teachers that men should be concerned with affairs outside the house inadvertently gave women considerable sway over the household. As Birge explains, "A widow had to hold the household together and ensure the survival of the family life. It was in the capacity of widow that women might gain total responsibility for a household's income and expenditure" (30).

Confucianists were particularly approving of the widow who remained chaste following the husband's death, thus, showing herself an example of loyalty.

During the tenth century, women from the upper classes suffered greatly from the practice of foot-binding. This crippled women more than in a physical way; it also hampered their creativity. By the Ming and Qing dynasties, however, poets and painters had begun to emerge. Though the process of acceptance seems to have been quite long, "Finally, in the seventeenth century, women were accepted as professionals and the sale of their artworks was regarded as an honorable means of livelihood" (Brown 249). Among the most illustrious names of women painters is that of Tang Souyu who was the wife of a highly-accomplished scholar in Hanzhou. Another was Guan Daoshen (Yuan Dynasty), who was accomplished as both a calligrapher and painter of bamboo (1262-1368), and was the wife of Zhao Mengfu, another painter and calligrapher (Giskin and Walsh 77).

Biographical encyclopedias that focused on women artists categorized such accomplished women according to whether they were palace ladies, wives and daughters, concubines, or courtesans. Nevertheless, they were not nameless.

Patient cultivation, emulation, practice, and even solitude might all contribute to why someone might excel to the point of having their work admired from generation to generation. The existence of such masters within the Confucian world suggests that the aspect of individuality that allowed people to choose for themselves the development of artistic skill, whether in painting, playing the zither, or otherwise, was very much a reality in that world.

In the next chapter, the rich legacy of Confucian art and creativity is discussed against the backdrop that great artists do not reach their high levels of achievement merely by a stroke of luck.

*Notes*

# CHAPTER 12
# CONFUCIANISM AND CREATIVE AUTONOMY

High artistic attainment of any kind (painting, playing an instrument, dance, and others) requires a great deal of dedication, and thus a measure of control over what one wants to do with one's time. It also requires autonomy if the would-be artist is to decide in what direction to take their creative endeavors. As Gimbutas points out, artists have often both been branded individualistic and "shown to be agents of society and humanity" (Gimbutas xi). This is not surprising because, for many kinds of art, it is not simply a matter of the blooming of spontaneous talent; the artist invests copious amounts of time, reflection, and practice, to produce works that might stand the test of time. To suggest that people who can so develop their skills and abilities had no sense of autonomy is to reject thousands of years of human experience. As Hulatt writes, "In viewing the artist as autonomous, we are asserting that the artist's activity is not determined by any extra-aesthetic influence" (6). The artist summons whatever impulses and sensations lie within and without in service of their creative works; to do so, year after year after year, requires the fortitude to carve out some space for oneself in a world where there might be endless demands upon one's time and attention.

Some of those who attained high positions in Confucian China on account of their having proven themselves masters of the Confucian canon and obtained positions in government as leaders, often continued to develop themselves not only in terms of mastery of ancient texts but in the development of their artistic skills. The high caliber of some of the artistic works that such individuals produced suggests that they did not allow themselves to be only consumed by their official duties. Rather, it seems that they were able to make time for the nourishment of their souls through their pursuit of art.

Just as memorization and emulation were part of the study of the classics, it might not be surprising to find that some of the paintings that the literati class devoted themselves to are said to have lacked originality. But even in such cases, one could not discount the individuality inherent in taking the time to do what makes one happy. The effort to compress and capture several kilometers of varied landscape onto a small patch of silk, as sinologist Michael Sullivan notes, enhanced "their growing awareness as creative individuals" (Sullivan, The Birth of Landscape Painting xiii). The willingness to first emulate other masters, the repeated attempts, the trial and error, and eventually, the creation of pieces to which they were willing to append their names, all show how much they wanted to leave something of beauty in the world.

The landscape paintings that were done by scholar-officials did not always attempt to capture the landscape in its rawness. Rather, the process required reflection and a personal touch to attempt to depict the landscape in abstract format (Wen and White 5). It must be noted that the practice of Chinese landscape painting spanned almost 1,500 years, through which it was affected by many different philosophies. But Taylor emphasizes that,

If we think of a standard East Asian landscape painting, we see mountains, mist, perhaps a waterfall, a river, a lake, or a small pavilion with a diminutive person. Such views are said to represent the infinity of time and space, the vastness of nature, and the smallness of humankind. Such qualities are considered Buddhist or Taoist—certainly not Confucian. Yet these paintings, called *wen-jen hua*, or literati painting, are very often the products of Confucians! (92)

In many cases, the literati who painted the landscapes or other subject-matter also wrote a few lines of poetry (Wen and White 5) or their names, to indicate not only some personal sensibilities but perhaps, the stamp of their individuality.

Throughout the centuries, in various dynasties, individuals distinguished themselves as painters of the first-rate even though for many of these, painting was an avocation, something to while away the time. Munsterberg reports that landscape painting became particularly prominent during the T'ang period (618-907 AD), a period that was dominated by four great artists.

Different parts of China evolved their own styles, giving rise to the Northern school and the Southern school. According to Munsterberg, "the motivation for classing some painters in the one school and some in the other is not based so much upon stylistic criteria as on the question of whether the artists were professionals or gentlemen-painters, the latter being the ones who were most admired" (52). A few notable names from the Northern Sung period include Tung Yuan, Chu-jan, Kuo Hsi, and Mi Fei (52), all of which confirm that the pursuit of individual excellence, retreat into isolation for creativity or rejuvenation, attention and focus on one's leisurely pursuits, were all very much a part of the Confucian way of life.

Quite apart from landscape painting, there have been other artistic pursuits that were encouraged for the training of those who sought to become gentlemen. One such pursuit was calligraphy, which was held in very high esteem (Taylor 87), with the works of calligraphy masters being studied in detail to unearth their secrets.

In fact, "The great masters of calligraphy have always been singled out for particular recognition and praise" (87).

To reach the heights of artistic excellence that resulted in garnering a large following, these masters must have devoted considerable time in solitude or been supremely focused. And further evidence of the recognition of individualism lay in the attention that was bestowed upon such individuals, some of whose names have continued to shine through even to this day.

# Notes

# CHAPTER 13
# CHALLENGES TO THE CONFUCIAN NOTION OF INDIVIDUALISM

In an earlier chapter, it was established that some of the leading proponents of Confucianism, including Mencius and Xunzi, and the writer of *Zhongyong*, Zisi, had different conceptions of the nature of the human being, that is, whether people are naturally good or that they have to be pushed into expressing morally upright behavior. The Grand Academy of the State was established as far back as 124 BCE at the capital (Yao and Yao 50) to seek out the best scholars to be incorporated into government service. Throughout the decades, Confucianism vied with a range of ideologies that both challenged and influenced it. For example, the Mohists and Taoists did not see Confucianism as being individualistic enough.

The Mohists, who frequently opposed the Confucianists were even more strident in their belief that individuals needed to exercise their rational and cognitive faculties to make decisions for themselves and not to follow the dictates and rituals of Confucianists (Brindley 12). The Mohists were not against self-cultivation in the form of knowledge acquisition but they wanted their followers, in a sense, to think for themselves, and to not be tied so strongly to ritual and the conformism that seemed to be a part of Confucian self-cultivation. In this respect, Mohism, founded by Mo Tsu (c. 470-391 BC), also known as Mo Di, Mozi, or Master Mo, was a bit more radical than Confucianism in insisting on individuals charting their own path. The Mohists also used step-by-step argumentation after the fashion of Socrates, which made them formidable opponents to contend with in their verbal contests with Confucianists.

No wonder then, that, Mencius, one of the leading lights of Confucianism "singled out the philosophy of Mozi as being among its most dangerous rivals" (De Bary and Bloom, Sources of Chinese Tradition 64). The Mohists identified with working people, that is, artisans and small property owners or merchants, and viewed Confucianists as "pretentious aristocrats who stand very much on their own dignity and on ceremony" (64). The Mohists agreed with Confucianists that government positions ought to be occupied by those most qualified to discharge the duties. They also agreed with the Confucianists that all human beings are equal. But, on the question of their perception of personal agency, they believed in taking action, including personal involvement, even to the point of endangering themselves, to bring about universal peace and harmony. Confucianists, on the other hand, were not eager to solve problems through personal agitation. The Mohists thus condemned the kind of individuality or sense of self-preservation that made people watch out for themselves rather than their fellow human beings; they argued that people who were universal in their love for others, and were willing to fight to protect others, were the superior ones. The Mohists saw Confucianists as being too partial or individualistic in the sense of prescribing "differences to be observed between close and distant relatives and between the honored and the humble" (75). The Taoists, for their part, believed that the Confucianists were not individualistic enough.

Some scholars point to Zhuang Zhou, who was at the Jixia Academy at the same time as Mencius, as the true founder of Daoism. The Taoists (Daoism), whose teachings are exemplified by the writings of Master Zhuang (Zhuangzi), were strong in their belief that individuals had to maintain a sense of agency. To this end, Zhuangzi is said to have tried to curtail the influence of state authority in the lives of the people. Daoism permeated Chinese life contemporaneously with various phases of Confucianism. The criticism of the Mohists and Daoists towards Confucianism made it seem that the individual living under a Confucian system was a highly-repressed soul who labored under the dictates of a hierarchy and was constrained by the obligations and duties to family members. Xu Keqian reports that researcher Chad Hansen believes that this lack of individualism is not just lacking in Confucianism but the Chinese culture and language as a whole (Keqian 446). Keqian, however, disagrees with Hansen, noting that if indeed it were the case that in the Chinese framework a person had only to be a part of the whole to be complete, then, "the individual would have never been complete and perfect when it was separated from that 'whole'....However, this is not the case, at least in the Zhuangzi" (448).

The argument that Xu Keqian marshals, from the Zhuangzi, is that, "the perfection and completeness of an individual's personality, or the ideal status of the individual spirit are more likely achieved in separation and loneliness" (448). This goes against Chad Hansen's contention that there was no sense of individuality in Chinese culture as a whole and Confucianism in particular. The strong attraction to the individual who can remain apart from the rest is further exemplified in the discovery that "Zhuangzi admires a lofty man who is different from the common people, for 'alone (*du*) he will come, alone (*du*) he will go. He may be called a man with uniqueness (*du*)'" (448). This strong predilection towards the kind of individualism that is not afraid to remain apart, even as a hermit, is associated with Daoism, not Confucianism. In *Zhuangzi*, we see an individuality that is much less caring of the larger society compared to Confucianism. Even so, in neither one, Daoism or Confucianism, was a person subjected to the dictates of society to the point of being crippled, metaphorically speaking.

One area in which the Daoists broke firmly with the Confucianists was in the matter of education. The Daoists believed in living naturally and eschewing rules and guidelines as well as cultural and ceremonial activities, whereas the Confucianists "believe that education and learning are required to alter the natural course" (Littlejohn 64). Daoists considered individuals to have their unique characteristics, which is that individuals were "changing and unique beings rather than fixed and interchangeable 'atoms'" (Keqian 445). Confucianists, on the other hand, believed in self-cultivation and used the metaphor of carving oneself as though one were a fine jade to represent the notion of self-cultivation. "The image of choice in Daoism is very different. In its texts the disciple should become like uncarved wood" (Littlejohn 66). Daoism did not encourage reason, study, or even leadership (67). It seemed like a freewheeling philosophy in which the wise could be found as much among the unwashed masses as among the so-called elites.

By the first century BCE, some Confucian scholars had begun to absorb Daoist ideas, especially the religious bent of Daoism. The notion that one could connect with the Dao, "the source of all being, the governor of all life, human and natural, and the basic, undivided unity in which all the contradictions and distinctions of existence are ultimately resolved" (De Bary & Bloom Sources of Chinese Tradition 78) without commitment to endless study and discussion must have seemed appealing to some people.

Confucianism was in opposition to another school of thought, Legalism, which emphasized the use of law and punishment in regulating the affairs of society. Confucianism believed that when people are guided by law and punishment, they will lose their sense of shame but that, if they are led by virtue, they will become good. Confucius wanted society to cure its ills by looking at the root of the issue and correcting the growth of the plant from seed through seedling to its flowering and beyond. Confucius said, "In hearing lawsuits, I am no better than others. What is imperative is to make it so that there are no lawsuits" (Confucius 12:13).

Confucianism believed in teaching young people from a young age to choose the path of rectitude rather than waiting until it was too late and punishing them for their mistakes or misdeeds. Confucianism was not a dictatorship. Its power lay in its influence, believing that each individual could weigh instruction on what was right and what was wrong and decide that it was better to follow the path of morality. By leaving room to the individual to decide what course to take, Confucianism unwittingly left room for rascals and scoundrels to materialize. This state of affairs raised the level of support to those who found law and punishment necessary, as with Li Si, a Legalist who became the architect of one of the most inhumane episodes of the Qin Dynasty, namely the burning of books (Fu 91) and the burial of scholars alive (91). The Legalists believed that Confucianism was too weak and too slow in shaping individual conduct and that the use of force was a much swifter instrument towards that end. Though the Legalists prevailed in controlling the society for a while, Confucianism was eventually restored and remained the dominant feature of Chinese life for over one thousand years. In its new incarnation, though, Confucianism did incorporate some features of legalism.

In recent decades, Chinese intellectuals who were eager to usher China into the modern world had much to criticize about Confucianism, including its supposed lack of individualism. It seems that the intellectuals of the May Fourth Movement needed something to blame after China had suffered one humiliation after another at the hands of Western powers. Perhaps, they saw the Confucian predilection towards harmony rather than a warlike posture as having been the reason why China was not prepared militarily to deal with the Western powers that imposed themselves on the country.

In an ironic twist, the same Confucianism that was blamed for the ills of society has now been rehabilitated and revived as the great pride of China, with Confucius Institutes being promoted by the Chinese government around the world as a symbol of China's ancient glory and modern advancement.

## *Notes*

# CHAPTER 14
# CONCLUSION

In this book, it has been argued that though indeed Confucianism has always valued harmony and community, it is a big leap to then say that there was no individualism in Confucianism. Not only was the subject of individualism itself a topic of discussion among Confucianists and other competing philosophies but also we see in the way of life of Confucianists various elements that equate with individualism, including the agency to choose what to do with one's life, and personal sacrifice in the long, hard years it took to master a large body of knowledge. Confucianists also had to learn how to comport themselves and master various skills, such as rituals, calligraphy, poetry, painting, or the zither. All of these required that a person be able to make decisions to focus on their personal needs, though not towards selfish ends.

The political aspect that attempted to take individualism out of Confucianism can also not be discounted. Western scholars, such as Max Weber saw individualism as a lofty Western ideal and sought to prove, by comparing China with the West, that China was missing this superb element in their culture.

Lately, other researchers, including Henry Rosemont, Jr. and Michael Sandel of Harvard have found communitarianism to be a much better ideal and sought to use Confucianism and its link with communitarianism as a way to nudge Western nations to abandon unfettered individualism.

Confucianism certainly did not encourage the kind of individualism that would mean trying to feather one's own nest. At the same time, it did not encourage going all out to save the world and neglecting one's own needs. Confucianism promoted the middle way, which is to cultivate oneself as an individual to the very best of one's intellectual abilities and social conduct, but always to do so with an awareness of one's fellow human beings, so that harmony would reign, to the benefit of both the individual and the society at large.

# *Notes*

# WORKS CITED

Ames, Roger T. and Henry Rosemont, Jr. The Analects of Confucius: A Philosophical Translation (Classics of Ancient China). Ballantine Books, 2010.

Bell, Daniel A., editor. Confucian political ethics. Princeton University Press, 2010. Berthrong, John and Evelyn Berthrong. Confucianism: A Short Introduction. Oneworl Publications, 2000.

Béteille, André, et. al. "Individualism and equality [and comments and replies]." Current Anthropology, vol. 27, no. 2, 1986, pp. 121-134.

Birge, Bettine. Women, property, and Confucian reaction in Sung and Yüan China (960– 1368). Cambridge University Press, 2002.

Bockover, Mary I. "Confucianism and Ethics in the Western Philosophical Tradition II: A comparative analysis of personhood." Philosophy Compass 5.4 (2010): 317-325.

Brindley, Erica Fox. Individualism in Early China: Human Agency and the Self in Thought and Politics. University of Hawai'i Press, 2010.

Brown, Kerry. Berkshire dictionary of Chinese biography. Berkshire Publishing Group, 2017.

Chan, Alan KL. "Confucian ethics and the critique of ideology." Asian Philosophy, vol. 10, no. 3, 2000, pp. 245-261.

Cheng, Chung-ying. The Primary Way: Philosophy of Yijing. SUNY Press, 2020.

Cheng, Zhongying. New Dimensions of Confucian and Neo-Confucian Philosophy: Contemporary Allegory and the Search for Postmodern Faith. SUNY Press, 1991.

Confucius. The Analects. Annping Chin, trans. Penguin Books, 2014.

Coward, Harold, et al. Readings in eastern religions. Wilfrid Laurier Univ. Press, 2006.

Dawson, Miles Menander. The Ethics of Confucius: The Sayings of the Master and His Disciples Upon the Conduct of "the Superior Man". G. P. Putnam's Sons, 1915.

De Bary, William Theodore. "Neo-Confucian Individualism and Holism." Individualism and holism: Studies in Confucian and Taoist values, edited by Donald J. Munro. Univ. of Michigan, 1985.

De Bary, William Theodore. Asian values and human rights: A Confucian communitarian perspective. Harvard University Press, 1998.

De Bary, William Theodore. Learning for One's Self: Essays on the Individual in Neo-Confucian Thought. Columbia University Press, 1991.

De Bary, William Theodore. The trouble with Confucianism. Harvard University Press, 2009. De Bary, William Theodore, and Irene Bloom. Sources of Chinese Tradition, 2nd ed., vol. 1. Columbia University Press, 1999.

Doh Chull Shin. Confucianism and Democratization in East Asia. Cambridge University Press, 2012.

Eno, Robert. "Mencius, An Online Teaching Translation." Indiana University (2016).

Eno, Robert. "The Great Learning and The Doctrine of the Mean: Translation, Commentary, and Notes." IUScholarworks, 2016, http://hdl.handle.net/2022/23424

Fu, Zhengyuan. China's Legalists. ME Sharpe, 2016.

Gao, Ruiquan. "The Source of the Idea of Equality in Confucian Thought." Front Philos China, vol. 5, no.4, 2010, pp. 486-505.

Gimbutas, Zivile. Artistic Individuality: A Study of Selected 20th Century Artist's Novels. Xlibris Corporation, 2012.

Giskin, Howard, and Bettye S. Walsh, editors. An introduction to Chinese culture through the family. SUNY Press, 2001.
Goldin, Paul Rakita. Confucianism. Acumen, 2011.

Graham, Angus Charles. Two Chinese Philosophers: The Metaphysics of the Brothers Ch'êng. Open Court Publishing Company, 1992.

Helin, Jenny, et al., editors. The Oxford handbook of process philosophy and organization studies. Oxford University Press, 2014.

Ho, David YF. "Selfhood and identity in Confucianism, Taoism, Buddhism, and Hinduism: contrasts with the West." Journal for the theory of social behavioral, vol. 25, no. 2, 1995, pp. 115-139.

Hu, Shaohua. "Confucianism and contemporary Chinese politics." Politics & Policy, vol. 35, no. 1, 2007, pp. 136-153.

Huang, Junjie, et al., editors. The Book of Mencius and Its Reception in China and Beyond. Vol. 52. Otto Harrassowitz Verlag, 2008.

Huggins, Robert, and Piers Thompson. "The behavioral foundations of urban and regional development: Culture, psychology and agency." Journal of Economic Geography 19.1 (2019): 121-146.

Hulatt, Owen, editor. Aesthetic and artistic autonomy. A&C Black, 2013. Ivanhoe, Philip J. Confucian Moral Self-Cultivation. Hackett, 2000.

Keqian, Xu. "A Different Type of Individualism in Zhuangzi." Dao, vol. 10, no. 4, 2011, pp. 445-462.

Kim, Sungmoon. Confucian democracy in East Asia: Theory and practice. Cambridge University Press, 2014.

Kim, Sungmoon, editor. Confucianism, law, and democracy in contemporary Korea. Rowman & Littlefield, 2015.

Kim, Uichol et al., editors. Individualism and collectivism: Theory, method, and applications. Sage Publications, Inc, 1994.

Knoblock, John. Xunzi: A translation and study of the complete works. Vol. 1. Stanford University Press, 1988.

Knowles, Heather. Passport Series: Asia. Milliken Publishing Company, 2011.

Kolstad, Arnulf, and Nini Gjesvik. "Collectivism, individualism, and pragmatism in China: Implications for perceptions of mental health." Transcultural psychiatry, vol. 51, no. 2, 2014, pp. 264-285.

Lambert, Andrew. "From aesthetics to ethics: The place of delight in confucian ethics." Journal of Chinese Philosophy, vol. 47, no. 3-4, 2020, pp. 154-173.

Lee, Ming-huei. Confucianism: Its roots and global significance. University of Hawai'i Press, 2017.

Legge, James. The Chinese Classics: The She king; or, the Book of poetry. Vol. 3. Trübner & Company, 1876.

Legge, James. "The classic of Filial Piety (XiaoJing)." (1885): 465-488.

Legge, James. The Sacred Books of China. Abingdon-on-Thames, Routledge, 1855.

Leung, Kwok. "Beliefs in Chinese Culture." The Oxford handbook of Chinese psychology, edited by Michael Harris Bond, Oxford Library of Psychology, 2010, pp. 221-240.

Li, Chenyang. The sage and the second sex: Confucianism, ethics, and gender. Open Court Publishing, 2000.

Lim, Tae-Seop et al. "Holism: A missing link in individualism-collectivism research." Journal of Intercultural Communication Research, vol. 40, no. 1, 2011, pp. 21-38.

Littlejohn, Ronnie L. Confucianism. New York, NY: IB Tauris, 2011.

Lukes, Steven. Individualism. Ecpr Press, 2006.

Machan, Tibor R. "On economic individualism." Psychosociological Issues in Human Resource Management, vol. 4, no. 2, 2016, pp. 145-184.

Mann, Susan, and Yu-Yin Cheng, editors. Under Confucian eyes: Writings on gender in Chinese history. University of California Press, 2001.

Mühlhahn, Klaus. Criminal justice in China: A history. Harvard University Press, 2009.

Munro, Donald J. "Individualism and holism: Studies in Confucian and Taoist values." (1985). Munro, Donald J. The concept of man in early China. U of M Center for Chinese Studies, 2001.

Munsterberg, Hugo. Landscape Painting of China and Japan. Tuttle Publishing, 2011.

Ni, Peimin. "Rectify the heart-mind for the art of living: A "gongfu" perspective on the Confucian approach to desire." Philosophy East and West, vol. 64, no. 2, 2014, pp. 340-359.

Nuyen, Ahn Tuan. "Confucianism and the Idea of Citizenship." Asian Philosophy, vol. 12, no. 2, 2002, pp. 127-139.

O'Brien, John. "Individualism as a discursive strategy of action: Autonomy, agency, and reflexivity among religious Americans." Sociological Theory, vol. 33, no. 2, 2015, pp. 173-199.

O'Dwyer, Shaun. "For East Asian students, 'Confucius made me do it' no excuse. The Japan Times, 12 July, 2017.

Puett, Michael, and Christine Gross-Loh. The path: What Chinese philosophers can teach us bout the good life. Simon and Schuster, 2016.

Rainey, Lee Dian. Confucius and Confucianism: the essentials. John Wiley & Sons, 2010. Richey, Jeffrey L, editor. Teaching Confucianism. Oxford University Press, 2008.

Romar, Edward J. "Virtue is good business: Confucianism as a practical business ethics." Journal of Business Ethics, vol. 38, no. 1, 2002, pp. 119-131.

Rosemont, Henry Jr. Against Individualism: A Confucian Rethinking of the Foundations of Morality. Lexington Books, 2015.

Rosenlee, Li-Hsiang Lisa. Confucianism and women: A philosophical interpretation. SUNY Press, 2012.

Schuman, Michael. Confucius: And the world he created. Civitas Books, 2015.

Shils, Edward. "Reflections on Civil Society and Civility in the Chinese Intellectual Tradition." Confucian Traditions in East Asian Modernity: Moral

Education and Economic Culture in Japan and the Four Mini-Dragons. Edited by Tu Wei-ming, Harvard University Press, 1996.

Sim, May. "Confucian values and human rights." The Review of Metaphysics, vol. 67, no. 1, 2013, pp. 3-27.

Simmel, Georg. "Individualism." Theory, Culture & Society, vol. 24, no. 7-8, 2007, pp. 66- 71.

Slingerland, Edward. "Virtue Ethics, The Analects and the Problem of Commensurability." Journal of Religious Ethics 1 (2001): 97-125.

Stockman, Norman. Understanding Chinese society. John Wiley & Sons, 2013. Stoeckl, Kristina. Multiple modernities and postsecular societies. Routledge, 2016

Sullivan, M. The birth of landscape painting in China (Vol. 1). Univ of California Press, 1962. Tan, Charlene. Confucian Philosophy for Contemporary Education. Routledge, 2020.

Tan, Charlene. Confucius. A&C Black, 2014.

Tan, Charlene. "For group,(f) or self: Communitarianism, Confucianism and values education in Singapore." The Curriculum Journal, vol. 24, no. 4, 2013, pp. 478-493.

Taylor, Rodney Leon. Confucianism. Vol. 6. Infobase Publishing, 2014.

Tu, Weiming. "Confucian Humanism in Perspective." Front-Lit Studies China, vol. 7, no. 3, 2013, pp. 333-338.

Tu, Weiming. Humanity and Self-Cultivation: Essays in Confucian Thought. Boston: Cheng & Tsui, 1998.

Tu, Wei-ming. Way, learning, and politics: Essays on the Confucian intellectual. SUNY press, 1993.

Wang, Chenyu. "Confucian Selfhood and the Idea of Multicultural Education." Confucianism Reconsidered: Insights for American and Chinese Education in the Twenty-First Century. Edited by Xiufeng Liu and Wen Ma, State University of New York Press, 2018, pp. 183-202.

Wei, Yang. "Learning as Public Reasoning (gongyi)." Confucianism Reconsidered: Insights or American and Chinese Education in the Twenty-First Century, 2018, pp. 111-130.

Weiming, Tu, and Daisaku Ikeda. New horizons in eastern humanism: Buddhism, Confucianism and the quest for global peace. Bloomsbury Publishing, 2011.

Weixi, Hu. "On Confucian communitarianism." Frontiers of Philosophy in China, vol. 2, no. 4, 2007, pp. 475-487.

Wen, Xiaojing, & Paul White. "The role of landscape art in cultural and national identity: Chinese and European comparisons." Sustainability, vol. 12, no. 13, 2020, pp. 1-19.

Wong, David B. "Rights and Community in Confucianism." Confucian Ethics: A Comparative

Study of Self, Autonomy, and Community, edited by Kwong-Loi Shun and David B. Wong. Cambridge University Press, 2004, pp. 31-48..

Woods, Peter R., and David A. Lamond. "What would Confucius do?–Confucian ethics and self- regulation in management." Journal of Business Ethics, vol. 102, no. 4 , 2011, pp. 669- 683.

Wortham, Anne. Individuality and Intellectual Independence, 1 August, 1975 Foundation for Economic Education. Retrieved from https://fee.org/articles/individuality-and-intellectual-independence/

Yao, Xinzhong, and Hsin-chungYao. An introduction to Confucianism. Cambridge University Press, 2000.

Yu, Jiyuan. "The beginning of ethics: Confucius and Socrates." Asian Philosophy, vol. 15, no. 2, 2005, pp. 173-189.

Yuen, Mary Mee-Yin. "Religious/Cultural Ethics as Living Traditions." Berkeley Journal of Religion and Theology, vol. 2, no. 2, 2016, pp. 99-123.

Yushun, Huang. Life Confucianism as a New Philosophy: Love and Thought. Bridge 21 Publication, 2020.

# CHRONOLOGY OF CHINESE DYNASTIES

Legendary Emperors
Yao
Shun
Yu

| | |
|---|---|
| The Three Dynasties | |
| Xia | c. 1900 – c. 1600 BC |
| Shang | 1570- 1045 BC |
| Zhou | 1045-221 BC |
|    Western Zhou | 1045 - 771 |
|    Eastern Zhou | 771 – 221 |
|       Spring and Autumn Period | 770-481 |
| Confucius – 551 – 479 BC* | |
|       Warring States Period | 481-221 |
|       Shi Huang Di – 259 – 210 BC | |
| Qin Dynasty | 221 – 207 BC |
| Han Dynasty | 202 BC – AD 220 |
|    Western Han | 202 – 9 AD |
|    Xin Dynasty | 9-25 AD |
|    Eastern Han | 25-220 AD |
| Three Kingdoms | 220-280 |
| Six Dynasties | 220-589 |
|    Wei | 220-265 |
|    Jin | 265-420 |
|    Northern and Southern Dynasties | 386-589 |
| Sui Dynasty | 581-618 |
| T'ang Dynasty | 618-906 |
| Five Dynasties | 907-960 |
| Song Dynasty | 960-1126 |
|    Northern Song | 960-1126 |
|    Southern Song | 1127-1279 |
| Yuan Dynasty | 1279-1368 |
| Ming Dynasty | 1368-1644 |
| Qing Dynasty | 1644-1911 |

*The above has been compiled from a wide variety of sources. They seem to be approximations.

# INDEX

Accomplished speakers, 138
Accomplishment, 48
Accusation, 118
Aesthetic, 109, 147
Alasdair Macintyre, 24
Aligning affairs, 48, 49
Aligning one's household, 48, 115
Allegiance, 81
Ambition, 38, 47, 54
Anger, 132
Anne Wortham, 88, 111
Anthropocentrism, 116
Aphorisms, 14
Apprentice, 132
Archery, 21, 50
Arrogant, 34, 54, 120
Artistic pursuits, 27, 150
Artistic skill(s), 145, 148
Authority figure, 118
Autonomous, 11, 15, 32, 109, 134, 147
Autonomous individual(s), 11, 109
Autonomy, 9, 25, 83, 102, 131, 147
Balancing the mind, 48
Ban Gu, 140
Ban Zhao, 140-143
Beauty, 132, 149
Beef, 120
Benevolence, 50, 57, 63
Benevolent and Wise, 138
Biographical encyclopedias, 144
Biographies of exemplary women, 138, 141
Blind, 34, 131
Book of Ceremonies, 22
Book of Changes, 22
Book of History, 22
Book of Odes, 22
Book of Rites, 99
Bowl of rice, 58
Boyu, 89, 131, 132
Bribes, 58
Brother Xiang, 34
Buddhism, 103, 104
Buddhist monks, 77
Building, 50, 81, 126
Burial(s), 112, 159
Calligrapher, 144
Calligraphy, 150, 151, 161
Canonical texts, 39
Cemetery, 112
Chad Hansen, 11, 156
Chaozhou, 104
Charity, 70
Charlene Tan, 14, 109
Charles Taylor, 24
Chaste and Obedient, 138
Cheng Hao, 26, 104
Child psychology, 42
Chinese culture, 11, 33, 156
Chinese framework, 156
Chinese history, 95, 103, 110
Chinese individualism, 91
Chinese intellectuals, 159
Chinese society, 9, 13, 28, 54
Choice(s), 9, 15, 25, 31, 47, 72, 92, 96, 100, 108, 111, 157
Christian priests, 77
Chu-jan, 150
Chuang Tzu, 134, 135
Civic organization(s), 116
Civil rights movement, 88
Civil service examination, 39
Classic of Changes, 22
Classic of History, 22
Classic of Music, 22
Classic of Poetry, 22, 73, 127
Classic of Rites, 22
Classics, 22, 35, 58, 84, 134, 148

Coercion, 15, 25, 105
Collaboration, 45
Coming to rest in the highest good, 48
Commitment(s), 14, 39, 45, 51, 82
Communitarian society, 14, 42
Communitarian value system, 14
Communitarianism, 9, 12, 15, 24, 100, 162
Communities, 31, 108, 128
Community leaders, 77
Comprehensive Discussions in the White Tiger Hall, 140
Conflict(s), 54, 142
Conformity, 89
Confucian China, 31, 42
Confucian classics, 84
Confucian ethos, 70, 105
Confucian humanism, 39
Confucian self-cultivation, 154
Confucian society/societies, 9, 12, 27, 28, 40, 41, 42, 43, 47, 89, 108, 113, 123, 137
Confucian world, 15, 84, 137, 144
Consideration, 30, 50, 62, 68, 69, 70, 78, 82, 115
Contentious, 120
Contradiction(s), 32, 158
Corrupt, 98, 130, 131
Corrupt government, 130
Cosmic authority, 58, 101
Cosmic relationships, 32
Counselors, 21, 123
Courtesy, 92
Creativity, 139, 144, 145, 150
Crime, 64
Criminality, 64
Cultural refinement, 66
Dance, 21, 147
Dao, 46, 57, 58, 65, 71, 80, 131, 133, 158
Daoism, 16, 104, 155, 157, 158
Daoist philosopher, 134
Daoist philosophy, 132
Daughter(s), 72, 115, 127
Daxue, 22, 45
Decision-making, 15, 83, 112, 135
Dedication, 44, 53, 147
Defiance, 120
Dependence, 11, 32
Depraved favorites, 138
Desire(s), 53, 57, 63, 64, 65, 80, 89, 131, 133
Determination, 28, 53, 100
Dignity, 101, 132, 154
Diplomat, 75
Disaster, 30
Discernment, 57, 85, 124
Discourse, 61
Discreet, 71
Discretion, 25, 92
Discrimination, 38
Disgrace, 70, 130, 133
Distinction(s), 32, 43, 123, 158
Divination, 21
Docility, 142
Doctrine of the mean, 14, 22, 46, 95, 99, 110
Dogmatic behavior, 76
Duke of Zhou, 20
Education, 14, 22, 40, 43, 44, 45, 53, 97, 102, 104, 112, 123, 138, 157
Educational opportunity, 40, 44
Egocentrism, 42
Egoism, 100, 116
Egoistic, 49, 73
Egotism, 35
Eight stages of practice, 48
Empathy, 60
Emperor Han Hedi, 140
Emperor Shun, 19

Emperor Yao, 19
Emulation, 40, 132, 144, 148
Enemies, 77, 98, 126
Enlightenment Europe, 16
Envy, 64, 97
Equality, 15, 25, 37, 38, 40, 43, 44, 120, 140
Equality of opportunity/opportunities, 38, 40, 43
Ethical examples, 77
Ethical living, 19
Examination(s), 26, 39, 44, 113, 133
Excellence, 60, 63, 85, 108, 128, 133, 150, 151
Exemplar(s), 20, 78, 143
Exemplary person(s), 21, 63, 89, 94, 127, 132, 133, 134
Exorcism, 76
Factions, 54, 127
False modesty, 35
Feminine virtue, 141
Filial piety, 22, 50, 70, 71, 79, 104, 119
Five cardinal relationships, 12, 123
Flexibility, 78, 79
Foot-binding, 140, 144
Fortitude, 58, 148
Fraternity, 104
Freedom, 25, 47, 88, 102, 103
Friendship, 79, 80, 81
Funeral, 142
Gaozi, 91, 92, 105
Geomancy, 22
Georg Simmel, 25
Gift-giving, 74
Good habits, 82
Gourd of water, 58
Grace(s), 91, 133
Grand academy of the state, 153
Grassroots, 33

Great Learning, 14, 22, 45, 48, 49, 90, 95, 96, 115, 124
Greed, 54, 63, 64, 97, 105
Greedy, 63, 134
Greek philosophers, 77
Gu, Ban, 140
Guan Daoshen, 144
Habits of mind, 54, 128
Han dynasty, 35, 140
Han Fei/Feizi, 101, 102, 105
Han Yu, 103, 104
Hansen, Chad, 11, 156
Harmony, 11, 12, 15, 38, 51, 56, 62, 73, 74, 80, 89, 120, 123, 128, 131, 135, 141, 142, 155, 159, 161, 162
Harvard, 9, 162
Hate, 97
Hattori Unokichi, 129
Heart-mind, 91, 92
Heartache, 142
Hedonism, 42, 100
Hereditary privilege(s), 122, 135
Hermit(s), 62, 135, 156
Hierarchy, 15, 120, 122, 124, 134
Hippocratic oath, 60
History, 19, 38, 59, 103, 110, 139, 140
History of the Farmer Han, 140
Holism, 31
Honesty, 20, 104
Hsiao Ching, 22, 70, 71, 118
Hsun Tsu, 91, 93, 95, 105
Hu Weixi, 14
Human agency, 15, 28, 70, 101, 135
Human ego, 119
Human excellence, 60
Human ingenuity, 97
Human relationships, 12
Humaneness, 50, 57, 59, 62, 63, 66, 129

Humanism, 39
Humanity, 50, 59, 60, 78, 97, 147
Hypocrisy, 35
I Ching, 22
Immorality, 95
Imperial Historian, 140
Infighting, 42
Independence, 32, 61, 113
Independent person, 131
Individual agency, 9, 15, 32, 33, 50, 72, 75, 125
Individual ambition, 47
Individual intellectuals, 33
Individual obligations, 13, 16
Indoctrination, 28
Inflexibility, 77
Initiative, 32, 75, 78, 105
Injustice, 132
Insight(s), 30, 124, 126
Intellectual ability/abilities, 39, 162
Intellectual curiosity, 67
Intellectuals, 33, 137, 159
Intelligence, 124
Investigation, 84
Islamic mullahs, 77
Isolation, 60, 62, 113, 150
Japan, 39
Japanese sinologist, 129
Jewish rabbis, 77
Ji Kangzi, 64
John O'Brien, 27, 31
Junzi, 40, 43, 46, 54, 59, 62, 63, 74, 77, 94, 95, 130, 132, 133
Junzi ru, 21
Keqian, Xu, 156
Key ideas, 18
Kim Sungmoon, 109
Kim, Uichol, 42
Kindness, 30, 92, 124
King Wen, 20
Kingly succession, 20
Kings, 19, 31, 44, 56, 124

Klaus Muhlhahn, 117
Kuo Hsi, 150
Lamb, 79
Landscape painting, 149, 150
Law, 65, 97, 105, 117, 158, 159
Law enforcement, 117
Lawsuits, 158
Leadership, 34, 122, 126, 128, 157
Legacy, 39, 145
Legalism, 158
Legalist school, 102
Li Chi, 22
Li Si, 159
Literati painting, 149
Literati-official, 84
Literature, 19, 33
Liu Xiang, 138-140
Loneliness, 110, 156
Loyalty, 50, 51, 79, 81, 104, 144
Lukes, Steven, 25
Lute, 73
Machan, Tibor R., 108
Macintyre, Alasdair, 24
Making intentions germane, 48
Making one's 'bright virtue' brilliant, 48
Making the people new, 48
Management, 50, 124
Ma Rong, 34
Marriage, 25
Masses, 23, 43, 157
Master Gao, 92
Master Zeng, 89, 90
Master Zhuang (Zhuangzhi), 155
Master Zisi, 89
Material gain, 45
Matronly models, 138
Max Weber, 9, 16, 161
Maxims, 14, 85
May Fourth Movement, 137, 159

Memorization, 110, 148
Mencius, 14, 15, 22, 26, 28, 40, 63, 69, 90-97, 99-101, 103, 105, 112, 124, 137, 138, 140, 153, 154, 155
Menial jobs, 53
Mental tranquility, 113
Meritocracy, 15, 28
Mi Fei, 150
Michael Sandel, 9, 24, 162
Michael Sullivan, 148
Ming dynasty, 104
Mo Tsu, 154
Modesty, 19, 35, 85, 92, 141
Mohism, 16, 154
Moral agency/agencies, 91, 99
Moral and political rights, 61
Moral aspirations, 81
Moral behavior, 52, 92
Moral cultivation, 45, 95
Moral excellence, 108, 133
Moral intuitions, 95
Moral nature, 91
Moral perfectibility, 111
Moral principles, 31, 81
Moral teachings, 89
Muhlhahn, Klaus, 117
Music, 21, 22, 50, 80, 104, 132
Mutton, 120
Nepotism, 116
Noble people, 43
Noble person, 40
Non-Chinese, 21
Northern school, 150
Northern Sung period, 150
Obedience to authority, 32
Obligation(s), 13, 14, 16, 123, 156
Obstacles, 25
Oppressive system, 33
Ordering the state, 48
Originality, 148
Ox mountain, 95

Oxygen, 111
O'Brien, John, 27, 31
Pacifist, 126
Parents, 13, 62, 69, 70, 72, 73, 91, 95, 111, 115, 120, 125, 132
Parochialism, 116
Patient inculcation, 93
Peace, 48, 74, 103, 128, 129, 131, 155
Persistence, 39, 45, 46, 50
Personal agency, 154
Personal ambition, 38
Personal comfort, 110
Personal devotion, 45
Personal power, 101, 113
Personal pursuits, 37
Personal touch, 149
Personal transformation, 83
Persuasion, 102
Petty person(s), 21, 63, 89
Poetry, 21, 22, 70, 73, 127, 149, 161
Police officers, 43
Political ceremonies, 21
Pork, 120
Praise(s), 57, 91, 151
Prescription, 67, 124
Principled and righteous, 138
Privacy, 25, 26, 27, 116
Privatization, 27
Progress, 50, 53, 77, 81, 128
Proper behavior, 29
Propriety, 44, 50, 53, 54, 74, 78, 134
Proverbs, 14
Psychologist(s), 12, 44
Public affairs, 69
Public sector, 44
Public sphere, 117
Qi, 69
Qin dynasty, 95, 99, 159
Qing, 144

Quarrels, 76
Queens, 44
Rectitude, 58, 60, 63, 81, 158
Refining one's person, 48
Regalia, 76
Rejuvenation, 150
Religious rituals, 21
Ren, 50, 57, 58, 59, 60, 62, 63, 65, 66, 71, 74, 79, 129, 134
Respectful, 71, 74, 76, 78
Restraint, 44, 63
Rice, 58, 69, 93
Righteous life, 63
Rightness, 50, 126
Rites, 22, 67, 68, 74, 75, 79, 90, 97, 98, 99, 104, 142
Ritual(s), 21, 29, 31, 50, 51, 54, 74-78, 103, 123, 132, 134, 143, 154, 161
Ritual propriety/proprieties, 50, 74, 77, 78
Ritual training, 76, 77
Sacrifice(s), 28, 45, 47, 54, 75, 76, 79, 110, 142, 143, 161
Sage-king(s), 19, 97
Sages, 19, 29, 105, 133
Sandel, Michael, 9, 24, 162
Scholar-official(s), 26, 77, 84,
Self-abnegation, 100
Self-actualization, 27, 44
Self-analysis, 113
Self-centered, 73
Self-correction, 127
Self-cultivation, 9, 28, 29, 38, 42, 44, 47, 50, 51, 60, 96, 99, 105, 125, 139, 154, 157
Self-culture, 141
Self-deception, 29
Self-development, 15, 25, 26, 45
Self-direction, 27, 62
Self-examination, 113
Self-gratification, 42
Self-mastery, 110

Self-recrimination, 119
Self-reflection, 50, 82, 83, 139
Self-respect, 110
Self-sacrifice, 40, 50
Setting the world at peace, 48
Shame, 92, 99, 158
Shang, 19, 20
Shen, 22, 29
Sheng ren, 132
Shi ching, 22
Shu, 50, 82
Shu ching, 22
Shun of Yu, 34
Si-Meng, 90
Si-Meng lineage, 90
Sima Qian, 140
Simmel, Georg, 25
Singapore, 12
Sinologist, 129, 148
Social ladder, 123
Social power, 83
Sociologist, 25, 27, 88
Solitude, 9, 26, 110, 144, 151
Song dynasty (960-1279 AD), 104
Spiritual and emotional power, 139
Spiritual leaders, 77
Spring and Autumn Annals, 22
Spring and Autumn Period, 19, 20
Stamp of approval, 81
Steven Lukes, 25
Subordinate(s), 46, 120
Sui dynasty, 39
Sullivan, Michael, 148
Sung era, 143
Superior(s), 43, 82, 86, 155
Suppression of desires, 65
Suppression of ideas, 89
Tai Ying Chi, 93, 94
Talent(s), 9, 35, 44, 45, 139, 140, 142, 147, 151

Temptation(s), 54, 58
The Book of Ceremonies, 22
The Book of Filial piety, 22
The Book of History, 22
The Book of Odes, 22
The Classic of Changes, 22
The Classic of History, 22
The Classic of Music, 22
The Classic of Poetry, 22, 73, 127
The Classic of Rites, 22, 90
The Dao, 46, 57, 58, 65, 80, 158
The Great Learning, 14, 22, 45, 48, 49, 90, 95, 115, 124
The Hsiao Ching, 22, 70, 71, 118, 119
The Legalist School, 102
The Mohists, 153, 154, 155
The Original Way, 103
The Six Classics, 22
The Song period, 104
Tibor R. Machan, 108
Timeliness, 68, 69, 70
Traditions of exemplary women, 139
Tranquility, 113
Trust, 81, 82
Trustworthiness, 50, 81
Truth-telling, 81
Tsu, 29
Tu Weiming, 39, 116
Tung Yuan, 150
Tutelage, 45
Tzu, Chuang, 134, 135
T'ang period, 150
Uichol Kim, 42
Uniqueness, 35, 156
Upper echelons of society, 33
Violence, 92, 95
Warring States Period, 20
Water, 58, 66, 104
Wealth, 19, 64, 65, 133
Weber, Max, 9, 16, 24, 161
Weiming, Tu, 39, 116

Weixi, Hu, 14
Wen-jen hua, 149
Western concept, 28
Western scholars, 9, 16, 161
White Tiger Hall, 140
Wife, 12, 46, 72, 73, 123, 142, 144
Willow tree, 92
Willpower, 49
Wisdom, 18, 19, 30, 38, 50, 53, 61, 72, 73, 78, 85, 88, 89, 133
Womanly bearing, 141
Womanly virtue, 141
Womanly words, 141
Womanly work, 141
Women's rights, 143
Wortham, Anne, 88, 111
Worthy and enlightened, 138
Xi, Zeng, 80
Xiang, Liu, 138, 139, 140
Xie Zhaozhe, 84
Xin, 50, 81
Xing, 91
Xi'an, 20
Xu Keqian, 156
Xunzi, 91, 95-99, 101, 118, 140, 153
Yan Hui, 58, 131
Yang Zhu, 15, 100
Yao, Emperor, 19
Yi, 50
Yuan dynasty, 144
Yuzi, 71
Zai Wo, 71, 72
Zeng shen, 22
Zeng Xi, 80
Zengzi, 89, 119, 125
Zhao Mengfu, 144
Zhao, Ban, 140-143
Zhaozhe, Xie, 84
Zhi, 50, 85
Zhong, 50, 79, 86
Zhongyong, 22, 73, 89, 153

Zhou dynasty, 19, 20, 21, 58
Zhu Xi, 48, 84
Zhu, Yang, 15, 100
Zhuang Zhou, 155
Zhuangzi, 132, 155, 156, 157
Zigong, 79
Zisi, 22, 26, 89, 90, 140, 153
Zisi-Mencius, 140
Zither, 73, 145, 161
Zither-like instrument, 80
Zixia, 82, 129

# About the Author

Everett Ofori teaches Marketing, Management, Negotiation, and English for Specific Purposes (English Conversation, Medical English, Public Speaking, Business Writing, Medical Writing, etc.). Everett has conducted lessons or designed curricula for the following organizations.

Accenture
Actelion
Ageo Central Medical College, Saitama
Amazon Web Services (AWS)
Asahi Kasei
Asahi Soft Drink Research, Moriya
AXA
Bandai
Barclays
Becton Dickinson
Boston Consulting
Chugai
Coca Cola
Deutsche Bank
Disney Japan
ExxonMobil
Fujitsu
Goldman Sachs
Gore
Gyao
Hitachi Automotive
Hitachi Design
IIJ (Internet Initiative Japan)
ING
Janssen
JP Morgan
JVC Kenwood
Kistler
Marubun

McKinsey Japan
Mitsubishi (Shoji)
Mizuho Bank
Moody's National Institute of Land and Infrastructure Management, Tsukuba, Japan (NILIM)
Nihon Michelin Tire, Gunma Prefecture
Nomura
PwC Consulting, Japan
Quest
Rakuten
Recruit
RGA Japan
Sekizenkai Nursing School, Kanagawa
Sompo
Sumitomo
Summit Agro
Suntory
Tokyo International Business College, Asakusabashi, Tokyo
Toppan
Toyohashi University of Science and Technology
Yokogawa Meters and Instruments
Yokohama Child Welfare Vocational College (Hoiku Fukushi), Higashi Totsuka, Kanagawa

www.ingramcontent.com/pod-product-compliance
Lightning Source LLC
Chambersburg PA
CBHW050027130526
44590CB00042B/1977